Common Core State Standards

2nd grade- Lesson Plans

Language Arts & Math

Teacher's Life

www.myteacherslife.com

Table of Contents

Suggested Reading

Fiction

- The Adventures of Taxi Dog by Barracca
- Nim's Island by Orr
- Dear Max by Grindley
- Dogku by Clements
- Fox and His Friends by Marshall
- Painted Dreams by Williams
- Could You? Would You? by White
- My Dad's a Birdman by Dunbar
- Get Ready for Second Grade, Amber Brown by Danzinger
- It's Test Day, Tiger Turcotte by Flood
- Matilda by Dahl
- Brundibar by Kushner
- Virgie Goes to School with Us Boys by Howard
- Lassie Come-Home by Wells
- Paint the Wind by Ryan
- Velma Gratch & the Way Cool Butterfly by Madison

- The Chocolate Touch by Catling
- Little Toot by Gramatky
- The Puppy Sister by Hinton
- Atomic Ace (He's Just My Dad) by Weigel
- Duck for President by Cronin
- Dude, Where's My Spaceship by Greenburg
- My Father's Dragon by Gannett
- Space Station Mars by Souci
- The Water Horse by King-Smith
- Baseball Saved us by Mochizuki
- Cam Jansen series by Adler
- Tuff Fluff: The Case of Duckie's Missing Brain
- Marja's Skis by Pendziwol
- Poppleton in Winter by Rylant
- Chester by Watt
- Diary of a Worm by Cronin
- Diary of a Spider by Cronin
- Gator Gumbo by Fleming

Informational

- Earth by Adamson
- Jupiter by Adamson
- Frogs by Bishop
- Spiders by Bishop
- Sea Horse: The Shyest Fish in the Sea by Butterworth
- Jump! From the life of Michael Jordan by Cooper
- Young Pele: Soccer's First Star by Cline-Ransome
- Actual Size by Jenkins
- Almost Gone by Jenkins
- The Story of Charles Atlas, Strong Man by McCarty
- Barnun Brown: Dinosaur Hunter by Sheldon
- Dolphins by Simon
- The Secret World of Hildegard by Winter
- Abe Lincoln: The Boy Who Loved Books by Winters
- Kartchner Caverns by Lankin
- What Is Pollution? by Larkin
- 14 Cows For America by Deedy

- All Pigs Are Beautiful by King-Smith
- Corn Is Maize by Aliki
- Count Your Way Through China by Haskins
- Duke Ellington: The Piano Prince And His Orchestra by Pinkney
- From Seed To Plant by Gibbons
- How My Family Lives In America by Kuklin
- I Am Rosa Parks by Parks
- I Live In Tokyo by Takabayashi
- Nasreen's Secret School by Winter
- Ruby Bridges Goes To School: My True Story by Bridges
- The Story Of Ruby Bridges by Coles
- The Supermarket by Saunders-Smith
- A weed Is A Flower by Aliki
- Wild Tracks by Arnosky
- Wild,Wild Wolves by Milton
- Zipping, Zapping, Zooming Bats by Earle
- Aunt Clara Brown by Lowery

Poetry

- Beast Feast by Florian
- The Bug In Teacher's Coffee And Other School Poems by Dakos
- Runny Babbit by Silverstein
- Days Like This by James
- Dear World by Nado
- Don't Read This Book Whatever You Do by Dakos
- Fathers, Mothers, Sisters, Brothers: A Collection Of Family Poems by Hoberman
- Guyku by Raczka
- Hailstones and Halibut Bones by O'Neill
- I Am The Book by Hopkins
- Weather: Poems For All Seasons

Language Arts

RL 2.1 Lesson One

Title: 5 W's And An H

Topic: Remembering details

Objective of lesson: Students will answer the questions who, what, when, where, why, and how about a given text

Common Core State Standard used: RL.2.1: Ask and answer such questions as *who, what, where, when, why,* and *how* to demonstrate understanding of key details in a text.

Materials needed:

The True Story of the Three Little Pigs by J. Scieszka (or other text of choice)

Hand outline (or trace their own)

Time for lesson: 30-45 minutes

Lesson:

- Read the text to students aloud.
- Explain to students that there are six basic questions that need to be answered by all good stories. Hold up your hand and starting with the index finger list who, what, where, when, why, and how is the center (because how is the glue that holds the story together)
- Tell students they are going to answer these main questions about the story you just read.

- Have students cut out or trace a hand and label the fingers (sample included)
- Have students fill out the who, what, when, where, why, and how or the story that was presented.

Assessment: Grading should be based on students offering correct information for each question based on the story.

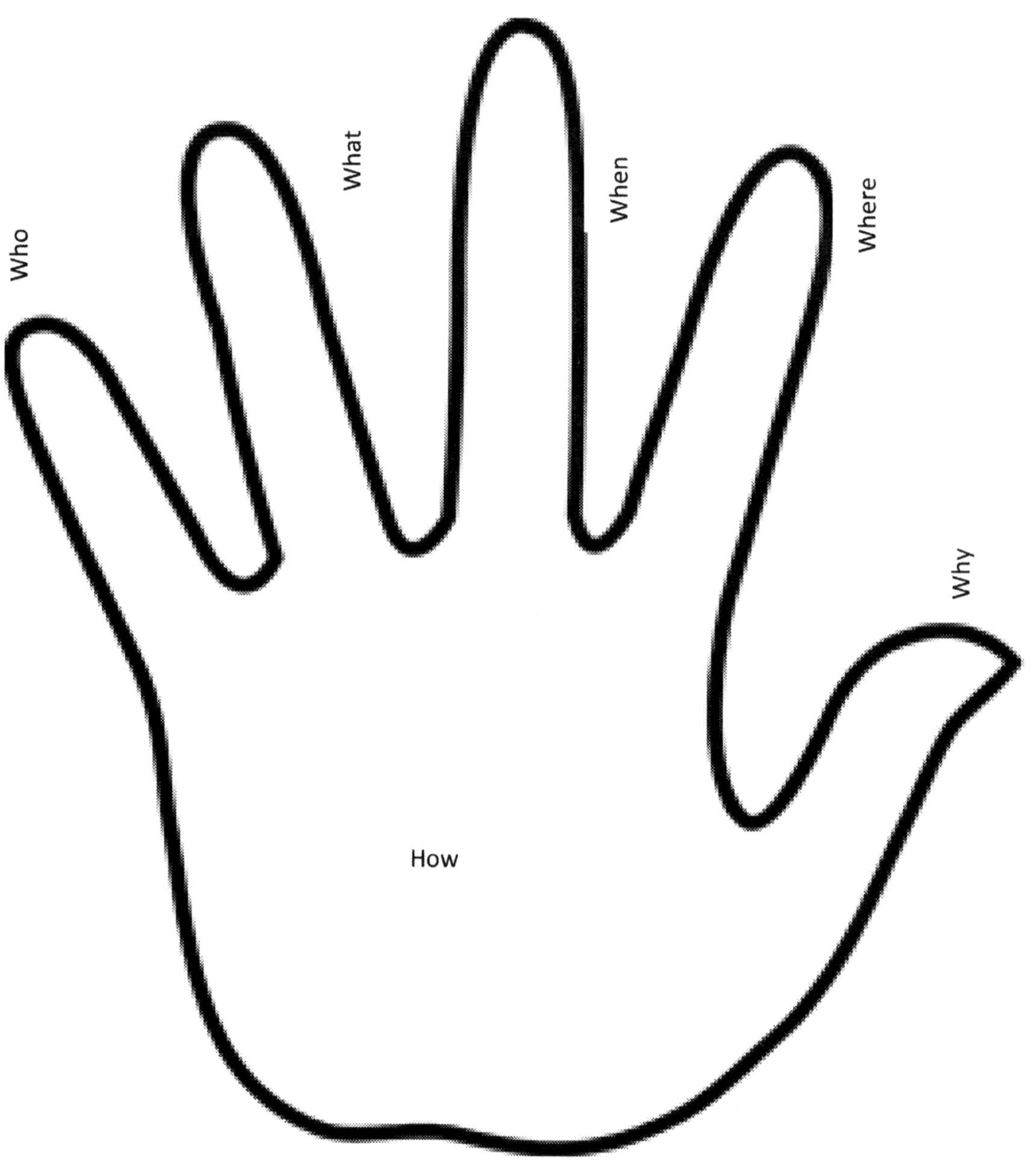

RL 2.1 Lesson Two

Title: Choose Me!

Topic: Remembering details

Objective of lesson: Students will answer the questions who, what, when, where, why, and how about a given text

Common Core State Standard used: RL.2.1: Ask and answer such questions as *who, what, where, when, why*, and *how* to demonstrate understanding of key details in a text.

Materials needed:

Popsicle sticks (about 50 depending on class size)

Text of choice

Time for lesson: 30 - 45 minutes

Lesson:

- Read the text to students aloud.
- Ahead of time, prepare 1 popsicle stick each with every child's name on it and place them in a cup. Also prepare several popsicle sticks with one question each on them (who, what, when, where, why, how). Place the sticks in two separate cups.
- Draw a student name out of the cup and have that student draw a question stick. Ask a specific question about the story using the key term the student drew.
- Wait for students to answer the question correctly.

Assessment: Grading should be based on student answering questions correctly.

*Popsicle sticks with student names written on are great for numerous activities and group choosing.

RL 2.2 Lesson One

Title: Tell Me Again

Topic: Remembering details in fables

Objective of lesson: Students will create drawings to represent the flow of a fable.

Common Core State Standard used: RL.2.2: Recount stories, including fables and folktales from diverse cultures, and determine their central message, lesson, or moral.

Materials needed:

The Olive Fairy Tale Book by Lang

Paper (or included comic strip paper)

Drawing or art supplies

Time for lesson: 45- 60 minutes

Lesson:

- Choose one or more of the stories from the collection to read aloud.
- Have students retell one of the stories through drawings (as in a comic strip). Remind students that telling a story in the correct order is very important, as are the details.

Assessment: Grading should be based on accuracy in retelling main events. Students should both accurately retell the story through drawings and retell in a sequential order.

Title: ____

RL 2.2 Lesson Two

Title: The Lesson Is...

Topic: Remembering details in fables

Objective of lesson: Students will discuss and list lessons learned from fables

Common Core State Standard used: RL.2.2: Recount stories, including fables and folktales from diverse cultures, and determine their central message, lesson, or moral.

Materials needed:

The Olive Fairy Tale Book by Lang (Copies of several different stories)

Sentence strips (One labeled -The lesson is...)

Time for lesson: 20-30 minutes

Lesson:

- Separate students into several small groups and provide each group with copies of a given fable from the text.
- Allow students to read and review the fable for their group.
- Have students list several lessons that could be learned from their fable.
- Allow groups to combine lessons or vote on lessons to create a single lesson learned from the fable.

- Choose one person from each group to write the lesson on a sentence strip and place it under the 'The lesson is…" strip.

Assessment: Grading should be based on accuracy of the group in creating a lesson that makes sense based on the story. Group participation should also be accounted for in the final grade.

RL 2.3 Lesson One

Title: What Happens When?

Topic: Describing character reactions to changes

Objective of lesson: Students will use a graphic organizer to describe character reactions based on a text

Common Core State Standard used: RL.2.3: Describe how characters in a story respond to major events and challenges.

Materials needed:

Graphic organizer (included)

Pencil/Markers

We are Best Friends by Aliki

Time for lesson: 50 - 60 minutes

Lesson:

- Read the text to the students aloud.
- As you are reading ask questions that lead students to guess how the two main characters will react.
- After reading, have students work in pairs or alone to fill out the graphic organizer listing how the characters react to given situations in the text. (List the situations for students)

Assessment: Grading should be based on accuracy in the reactions for each character.

Name______________________ Date______________

Character Traits

Write the name of the main character of your story in the banner at the top. Then write three traits the character possesses in the middle three boxes. In the bottom boxes, write examples from the book of the character demonstrating each of the three traits.

Title or Chapter____

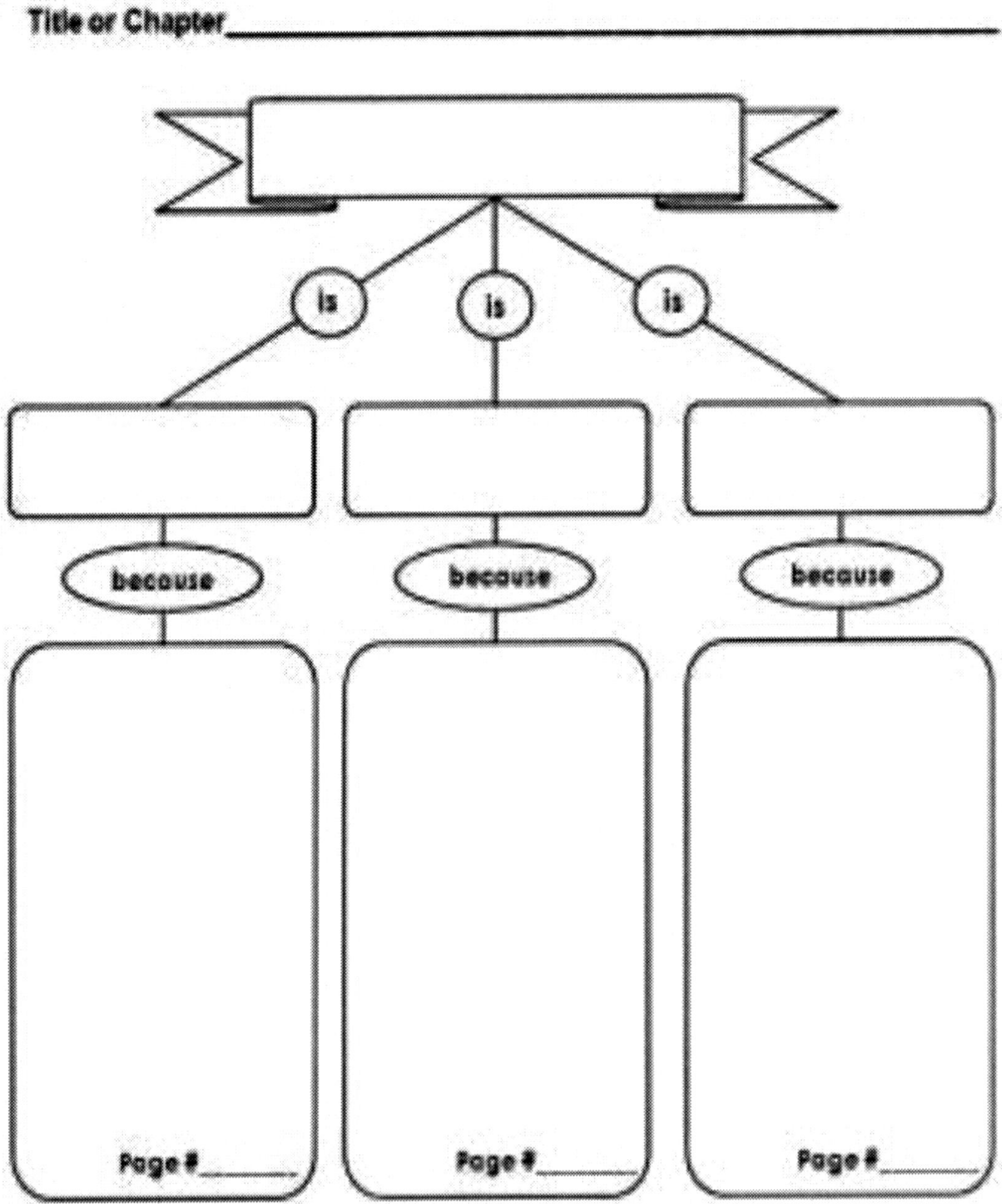

RL 2.3 Lesson Two

Title: I Think...

Topic: Describing character reactions to changes

Objective of lesson: Students will predict how a given character would react.

Common Core State Standard used: RL.2.3: Describe how characters in a story respond to major events and challenges.

Materials needed:

Junie B. Jones series (any text)

Paper

Art supplies

Time for lesson: 40 -50 minutes

Lesson:

- Read the text (or part of text) to the students aloud.
- Have students imagine Junie B, in a situation that is not in the book (ie Going to the doctor, getting caught in a lie, getting lost at the mall, etc)
- Have students draw a picture and write two to three sentences about how Junie B. would react. Remind students to base their guesses on how Junie B. has behaved in other situations.

Assessment: Grading should be based on accuracy in the reactions for a given character as well as appropriate pictures based on predictions.

RL 2.4 Lesson One

Title: I Feel __ After Hearing That.

Topic: Recognizing that how a poem is written and read can affect how the reader responds.

Objective of lesson: Students will recognize that rhyming patterns and nonsense words set the mood for a poem or set of poems.

Common Core State Standard used: RL.2.4: Describe how words and phrases (e.g., regular beats, alliteration, rhymes, repeated lines) supply rhythm and meaning in a story, poem, or song.

Materials needed:

Runny Babbit by Shel Silverstein

Face chain (Included)

Time for lesson: 30 - 40 minutes

Lesson:

- Read several poem choices from Runny Babbit
- Have students fold the expressions on the lines so they may present only one at a time.
- After reading a poem, have students choose the face that best describes how the reading makes them feel

Assessment: Grading should be based on participation and logical expression choices.

RL 2.4 Lesson Two

Title: Feel Those Beats

Topic: Hearing different beats and associating them with different moods.

Objective of lesson: Students will recognize that beats in reading or music can elicit different feelings.

Common Core State Standard used: RL.2.4: Describe how words and phrases (e.g., regular beats, alliteration, rhymes, repeated lines) supply rhythm and meaning in a story, poem, or song.

Materials needed:

Different types of music that is age appropriate (classical, African, lullaby, children's music (upbeat), etc)

Emotion word chain (Included)

Time for lesson: 30 - 40 minutes

Lesson:

- Listen to several music selections, one at a time with student emotion choices between each selection.
- Have students cut the emotion words on the lines so they may present only one at a time.
- After listening to a music selection, have students choose one word which best describes how that music made them feel.
- Ask students why certain selections made them feel that way.

Assessment: Grading should be based on participation and logical expression choices.

Happy	Sad	Excited
Angry	Sick	Tired

RL 2.5 Lesson One

Title: Chugging Along

Topic: Describing beginning, middle, and end of a story

Objective of lesson: Students will recognize and write out the parts of a story.

Common Core State Standard used: RL.2.5: Describe the overall structure of a story, including describing how the beginning introduces the story and the ending concludes the action.

Materials needed:

Train organizer (included)

Text of choice

Time for lesson: 45 - 60 minutes

Lesson:

- Read the chosen text to the class or small groups
- Explain to students that every story has a beginning, middle, and end. These are usually main events in the story. There is often more than one event in the middle, but only one beginning and end event.
- Work with students to write out the main events of a story (not necessarily in order)
- Allow students to identify the story parts by placing them in order on the train.

Assessment: Grading should be based on participation and on ordered events that are placed correctly on the train (beginning -engine, end-caboose)

*Add more cars as needed

RL 2.5 Lesson Two

Title: Wrap It Up

Topic: Concluding a story

Objective of lesson: Students will recognize and write out the parts of a story.

Common Core State Standard used: RL.2.5: Describe the overall structure of a story, including describing how the beginning introduces the story and the ending concludes the action.

Materials needed:

Sample story start

Paper

Pencil

Time for lesson: 45 - 60 minutes

Lesson:

- Read the provided passage (or one of your own) to students.
- Explain that the passage has no ending and their responsibility is to finish the story in a way that ties up all the problems.
- Allow students time to write.

Assessment: Grading should be based on creating an ending that makes sense and wraps up the given information.

Sample passage:

Once upon a time two children awoke early and ran downstairs to watch cartoons. At the bottom of the staircase sat a large colorful package. The oldest child, a boy, ran to read the tag. He read his name, Randy, and his sister's name Stacy. This meant the present must be for both of them. The pair immediately ran upstairs to ask their mother if it was alright to open the gift. As she assumed it was from their father who had left on business that morning, she said to go ahead.

The children ran back down the stairs and ripped into the colorful paper. Inside they each found a smaller box with their names engraved on the top. Each child opened the box to find a small scroll inside. As the scrolls were opened the same message was written on each. "To the one who opens this box three wishes are granted. Beware to the wisher, careful of your desires. Wishes are not as they always seem so make sure what you wish is really what you dream."

The children glanced at each other for a moment before running off to separate rooms. The little boy, who felt older and wiser, decided to make the first wish. He wished for all the best toys in the world. Instantly, his room filled with toys. It was so filled that he was pushed out and the toys so crammed in the room that he could not get even one out. The little boy instantly went to work to free toys.

Stacy, the little girl saw what happened and knew she had to be careful. She thought for several more minutes and knew what she wanted. She wished for a doll that was just like a real girl so she would always have someone to play with. Seconds later a doll appeared. It could walk, talk, eat, and play. Unfortunately all the doll girl wanted to do was talk and argue. Stacy was very upset at her wish. Stacy tried everything to get her new doll to be quiet, but finally she had enough. Stacy's second wish was used to make her life like doll disappear. Knowing she only had three wishes, Stacy made sure not to wish for anything else just yet.

While Stacy was sitting thinking about her third wish, Randy was still not making progress in getting into his overstuffed room. Randy was careful in his next wish. I wish we had a bigger house than this one, right in our backyard with all of our stuff neatly organized inside. Poof! The wish immediately came true and both children and the mother were whisked to the new house by magic. It was a large, beautiful house that had plenty of room and was filled with all of their worldly possessions. Randy was happy and began playing with his new toys immediately. His mother was shocked at first, but smiled continually as she explored the large new home. Each child had only one wish left and both knew it had to be used wisely.

Now, you finish the story. Make sure to wrap up all the loose ends.

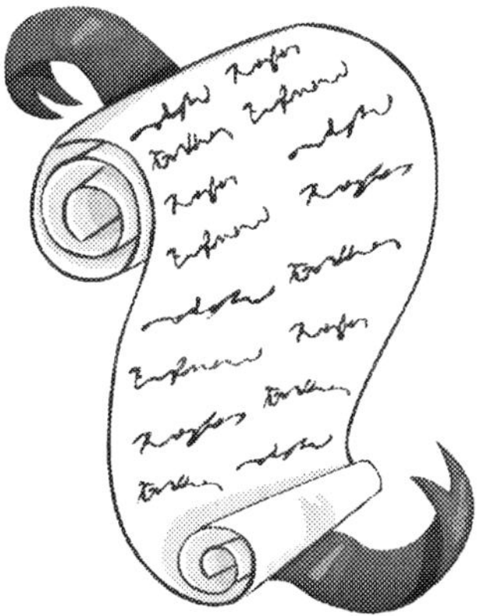

RL 2.6 Lesson One

Title: Read As If You Are...

Topic: Using different points of view

Objective of lesson: Students will read using different emotions no matter what the text calls for.

Common Core State Standard used: RL.2.6: Acknowledge differences in the points of view of characters, including by speaking in a different voice for each character when reading dialogue aloud.

Materials needed:

Popsicle sticks (at least 5 more if desired)

A text or short paragraph to read

Time for lesson: 30-45 minutes

Lesson: (Small groups or large groups are appropriate)

- Have students in the group pick a popsicle stick (Each stick will be labeled with one of the following words: Sick, sad, happy, excited, angry, etc)
- Have each student read the passage in a tone that the popsicle stick asks. i.e. Read as if they are sick or sad or angry...
- Have students discuss how the passage changes when the tone it is read in changes.

Assessment: Grading should be based on participation and accuracy in tone.

RL 2.6 Lesson Two

Title: Dialogue It

Topic: Using different voices to recognize different characters speaking

Objective of lesson: Students will read using different voices for different people

Common Core State Standard used: RL.2.6: Acknowledge differences in the points of view of characters, including by speaking in a different voice for each character when reading dialogue aloud.

Materials needed:

Short play with dialogue (Included)

Time for lesson: 30-45 minutes

Lesson: (Small groups or large groups are appropriate)

- Assign or have students choose parts based on the play
- Allow students to choose a voice which they feel is appropriate for their character
- Have students read each part as assigned

Assessment: Grading should be based on participation and accuracy in tone, as well as following and reading at appropriate times.

Caps For Sale

By Esphyr Slobodkina

Parts (10): Narrator 1 Narrator 2 Narrator 3 Narrator 4
Peddler Monkeys (5)

Narrator 1: Caps For Sale. A tale of a Peddler, Some Monkeys and Their Monkey Business.

Narrator 2: Once there was a peddler who sold caps. But he was not like an ordinary peddler carrying his wares on his back. He carried them on top of his head.

Narrator 3: First he had on his own checked cap, then a bunch of gray caps, then a bunch of brown caps, then a bunch of blue caps, and on the very top a bunch of red caps.

Narrator 4: He walked up and down the streets, holding himself very straight so as not to upset his caps. As he went along he called,

Peddler: "Caps! Caps for sale! Fifty cents a cap!"

Narrator 1: One morning he couldn't sell any caps. He walked up the street and he walked down the street calling,

Peddler: "Caps! Caps for sale. Fifty cents a cap."

Narrator 2: But nobody wanted any caps that morning. Nobody wanted even a red cap.

Narrator 3: He began to feel very hungry, but he had no money for lunch.

Peddler: "I think I'll go for a walk in the country,"

Narrator 4: said he. And he walked out of town-slowly, slowly, so as not to upset his caps.

Narrator 1: He walked for a long time until he came to a great big tree.

Peddler: "That's a nice place for a rest."

Narrator 2: And he sat down very slowly, under the tree and leaned back little by little against the tree-trunk so as not to disturb the caps on his head.

Narrator 3: Then he put his hand up to feel if they were straight- first he checked his own checked cap, then the gray caps, then the brown caps, then the blue caps, then the red caps on the very top.

Narrator 4: They were all there. So he went to sleep. He slept for a long time.

Narrator 1: When he woke he was refreshed and rested.

Narrator 2: But before standing up he felt with his hand to make sure his caps were in the right place. All he felt was his own checked cap!

Narrator 3: He looked to the right of him, No caps. He looked to the left of him. No caps. He looked to the back of him. No caps. He looked behind the tree. No caps.

Narrator 4: Then he looked up into the tree and what do you think he saw? On every branch sat a monkey. On every monkey was a gray, or a brown, or a blue, or a red cap!

Narrator 1: The peddler looked at the monkeys. The monkeys looked at the peddler. He didn't know what to do. Finally he spoke to them.

Peddler: "You monkeys, you! You give me back my caps."

Narrator 2: He said, shaking a finger at them. But the monkeys only shook their fingers back and him and said,

Monkeys: Tsz, tsz, tsz.

Narrator 3: This made the peddler angry, so he shook both hands at them and said,

Peddler: "You monkeys, you! You give me back my caps."

Narrator 4: But the monkeys only shook both their hands back at him and said,

Monkeys: Tsz, tsz, tsz.

Narrator 1: Now he felt quite angry. He stamped his foot, and he said,

Peddler: "You monkeys, you! You better give me back my caps!"

Narrator 2: But the monkeys only stamped their feet back at him and said,

Monkeys: Tsz, tsz, tsz.

Narrator 3: By this time the peddler was really very, very angry. He stamped both his feet and shouted,

Peddler: "You monkeys, you! You must give me back my caps!"

Narrator 4: But the moneys only stamped both their feet back and him and said,

Monkeys: Tsz, tsz, tsz.

Narrator 1: At last he became so angry that he pulled off his own cap, threw it on the ground, and began to walk away.

Narrator 2: But then, each monkey pulled off his cap...and all the gray caps, and all the brown caps, and all the blue caps, and all the red caps came flying down out of the tree.

Narrator 3: So the peddler picked up his caps and put them back on his head-first his own checked cap, then the gray caps, then the brown caps, then the blue caps, then the res caps on the very top.

Narrator 4: And slowly, slowly, he walked back to town calling,

Peddler: "Caps ! Caps for sale! Fifty cents a cap!"

All: The end.

RL 2.7 Lesson One

Title: Where Are We?

Topic: Recognizing setting based on print information only.

Objective of lesson: Students will use pictures as clues to the setting of a story

Common Core State Standard used: RL.2.7: Use information gained from the illustrations and words in a print or digital text to demonstrate understanding of its characters, setting, or plot.

Materials needed:

Picture groups (Included)

Time for lesson: 30-40 minutes

Lesson: (Small groups or large groups are appropriate)

- Give each student the sheet of grouped pictures
- Tell students that each picture group offers hints at a setting
- Have students write what they think the setting could be

Assessment: Grading should be based on accuracy in naming settings based on clues.

RL 2.7 Lesson Two

Title: What's Happening?

Topic: Understanding plot through illustrations

Objective of lesson: Students will determine plot based only on a snapshot scene

Common Core State Standard used: RL.2.7: Use information gained from the illustrations and words in a print or digital text to demonstrate understanding of its characters, setting, or plot.

Materials needed:

Scenes (Included)

Paper

Pencil/Marker

Time for lesson: 45-60 minutes

Lesson: (Pairs)

- Give each student pair one of the included scenes
- Explain to students that sometimes, if we do not understand what is going on in a story, we can look at the picture and figure it out.
- Ask students to create a story based on their scene
- Have students write out the story and share with another group or the class.

Assessment: Grading should be based on stories that apply to the given scene, group work, and presentation skills.

RL 2.9 Lesson One

Title: Compared To What?

Topic: Comparing and contrasting

Objective of lesson: Students will compare and contrast stories using a Venn diagram.

Common Core State Standard used: RL.2.9: Compare and contrast two or more versions of the same story (e.g., Cinderella stories) by different authors or from different cultures

Materials needed:

The Three Little Pigs by Mother Goose

The Three Little Javalinas by Lowell

Venn diagram (sample)

Time for lesson50-60 minutes

Lesson: (Small groups)

- Read both books to the group of students
- Show students a Venn diagram and explain that one side is for Javalinas, one for Pigs, and the center for things they share. Offer the example for the middle, there are three of both main animals as a center starter.
- Ask students to give an answer that will fit into one of the three categories and find out which category the answer falls into.

- Fill out or allow students to fill out the spot each trait of the story(ies) fall into.

Assessment: Grading should be based on participation and appropriate answers

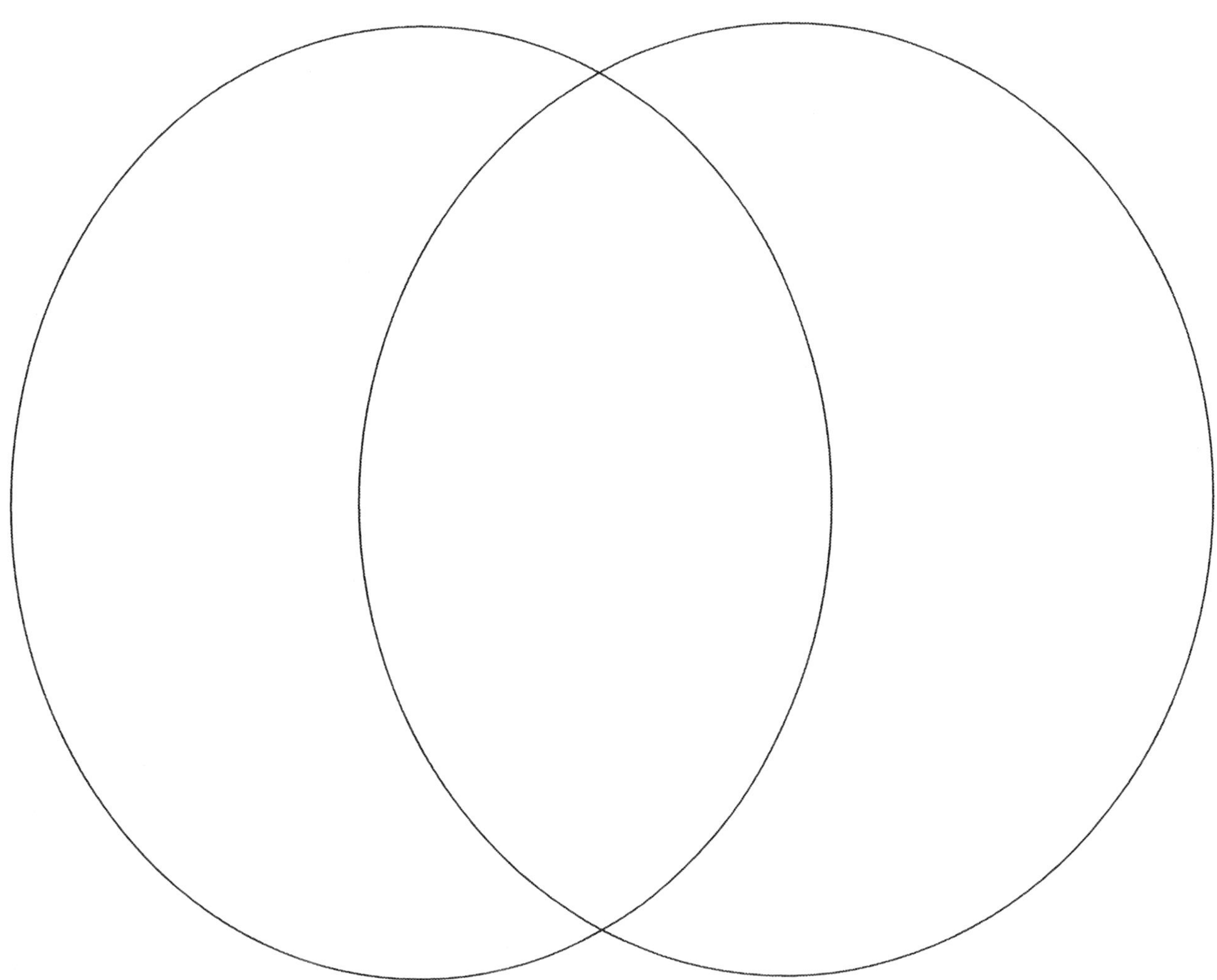

RL 2.9 Lesson Two

Title: Find The Differences

Topic: Comparing and contrasting

Objective of lesson: Students will compare and contrast stories

Common Core State Standard used: RL.2.9: Compare and contrast two or more versions of the same story (e.g., Cinderella stories) by different authors or from different cultures

Materials needed:

The Gingerbread Man

The Stinky Cheese Man by Scieszka

Time for lesson: 50-60 minutes

Lesson: (Large groups)

- Read both books to the group of students
- List only the differences in the stories on the board
- Allow everyone in class to try to guess something different
- Time permitting, show similar illustrations from each book and let students mark the differences

Assessment: Grading should be based on participation and appropriate answers

RI 2.1 Lesson One

Title: Keys To The Castle

Topic: Identifying key details

Objective of lesson: Students will identify the who, what, when, where, why, and how of an informational text

Common Core State Standard used: RI.2.1: Ask and answer such questions as *who, what, where, when, why*, and *how* to demonstrate understanding of key details in a text.

Materials needed:

Graphic organizer (Sample)

Pencil

The Flyer Flew! The Invention of the Airplane by Hill

Time for lesson: 45-60 minutes

Lesson:

- Share the text with students. Begin by saying that the text is true about the inventors of the airplane. Explain that details are very important in non-fiction or informational writing.
- Explain to students that they are going to use a graphic organizer to answer the six main questions: who, what, when, where, why, and how about the text.

- Explain that the tops give the questions and the castle towers allow students to write the answer. Castle towers can be connected by tabs to form a rounded shape that sets up.

Assessment: Grading should be based on the correct information being placed in the towers

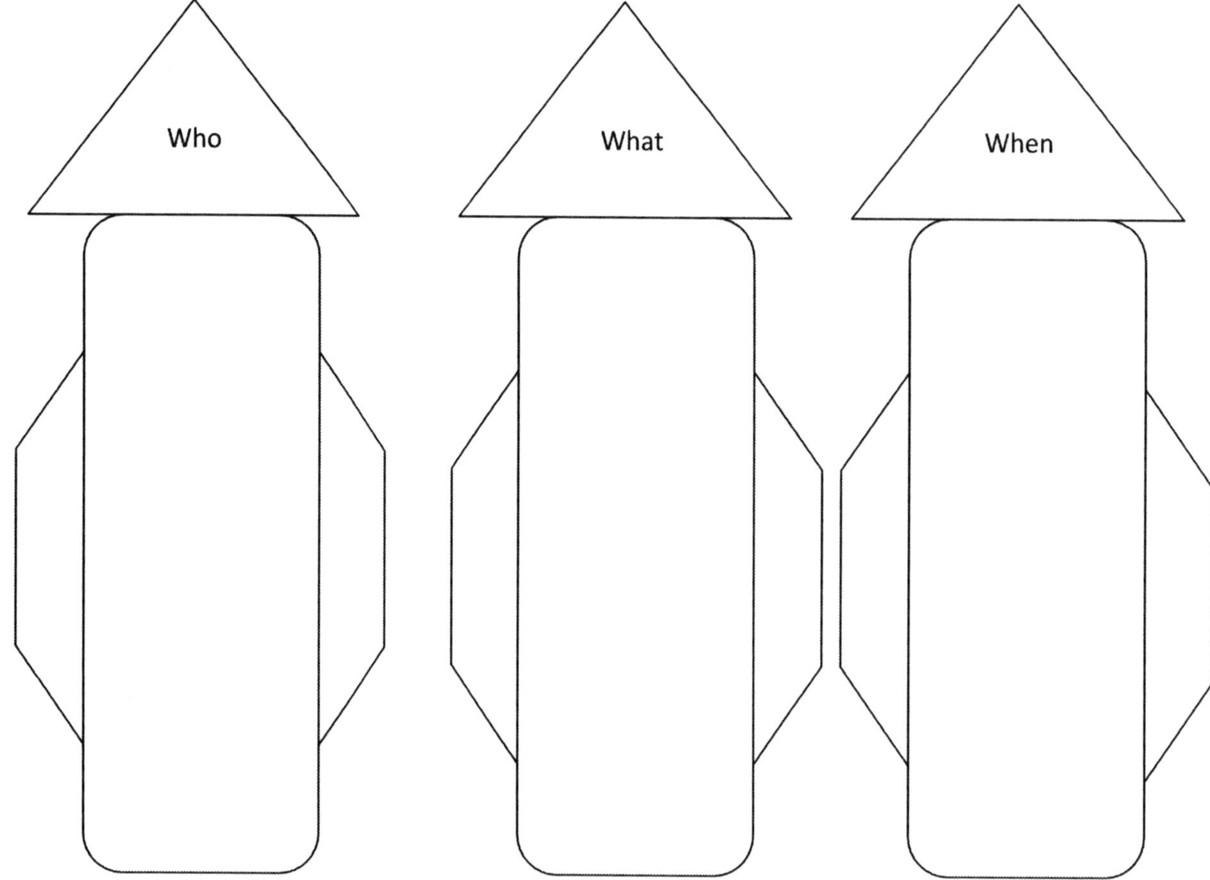

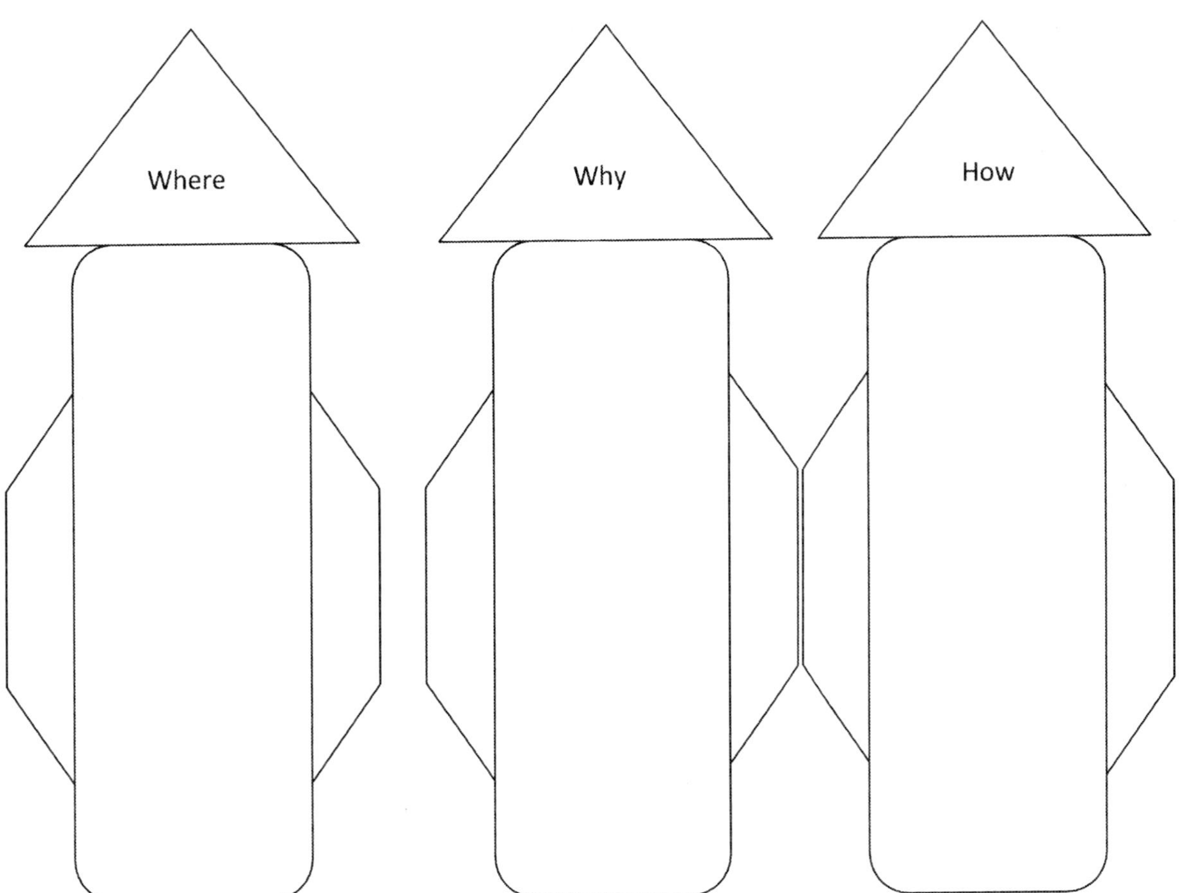
Where
Why
How

RI 2.1 Lesson Two

Title: Key Into Details

Topic: Identifying key details

Objective of lesson: Students will identify the who, what, when, where, why, and how in informational texts

Common Core State Standard used: RI.2.1: Ask and answer such questions as *who, what, where, when, why,* and *how* to demonstrate understanding of key details in a text.

Materials needed:

Graphic organizer (Sample)

Pencil

Pipe cleaners

Choice of informational text

Time for lesson: 30-40 minutes

Lesson:

- Explain to students that details hold the important parts of an informational text.
- Have students cut out the key shapes (included) and write each of the six 'key' detail questions on a key. Then punch a hole at the top of each key and string them onto a pipe cleaner (keychain) that can be twisted closed.

- As you read a text and come across a detail, have students hold up the key that explains that detail.

Assessment: Grading should be based on participation and appropriate answers

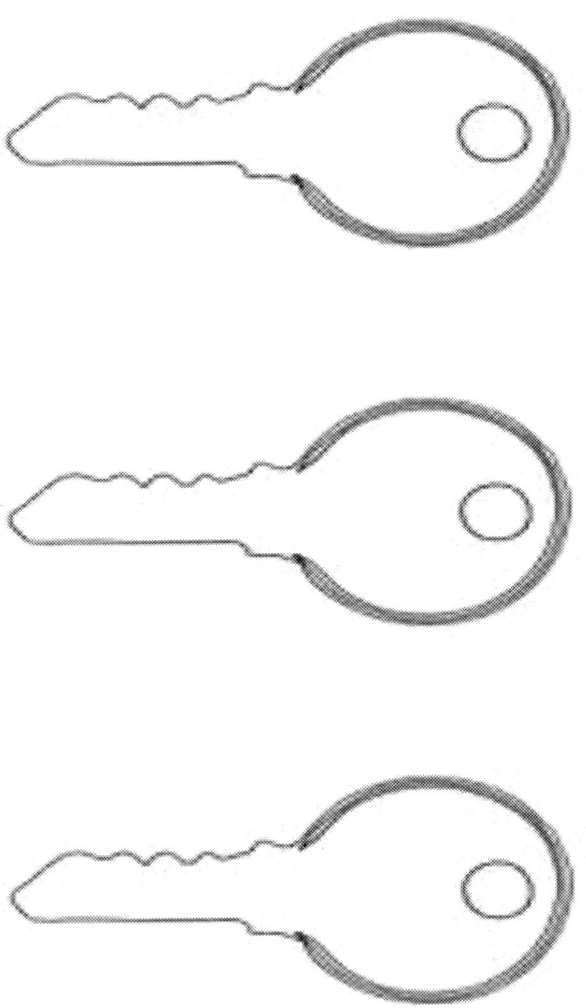

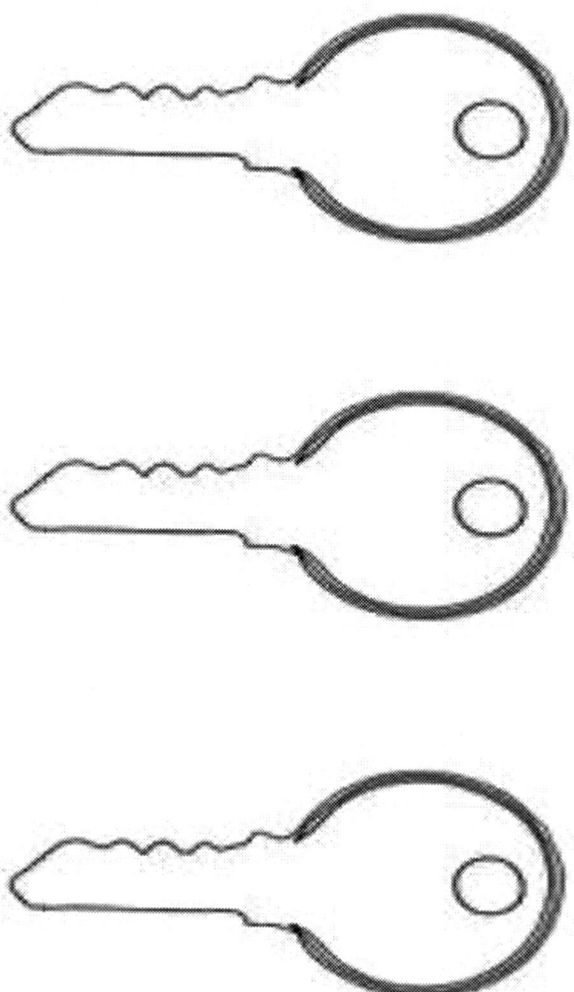

RI 2.2 Lesson One

Title: Just The Highlights Please

Topic: Identifying main topics

Objective of lesson: Students will identify main topics of informational texts

Common Core State Standard used: RI.2.2:Identify the main topic of a multi- paragraph text as well as the focus of specific paragraphs within the text.

Materials needed:

Choice of informational text (sample included)

Highlighting tape or sheet protectors and light colored dry erase markers

Time for lesson: 30-40 minutes

Lesson:

- Share the passage(s) with students. Explain that writing has one topic that is related to every sentence in the paragraph and whole passage. This topic is usually mentioned in the first or second sentence.
- Have students use highlighting tape to mark the main topic of a given passage.

Assessment: Grading should be based on marking appropriate main topics.

Sample Passage:

Sound can be measured by how high or low it is. This measurement is called pitch. An object or instrument that vibrates very slowly makes a sound with a low pitch. An object or instrument that vibrates very quickly makes a sound with a high pitch.

Have you ever listened to the instruments in an orchestra? The bigger an instrument is, the lower the sound that it makes. A tiny piccolo flute has a very high pitch, while a full-size flute has a much lower pitch. A violin's pitch is higher than a viola or bass. A trumpet's pitch is higher than a tuba's. Sound travels in waves. The vibrations from the instruments reach your ear, and you hear them as different sounds.

Volume is different than pitch. You can use more or less volume to make a sound, like music or your voice, louder or softer. Volume and pitch work together to make sounds sound the way that they do. Next time you hear an instrument play, listen to music, or even just listen to someone's voice as they talk or sing, see if you can hear the difference between the volume and the pitch.

RI 2.2 Lesson Two

Title: One Word

Topic: Identifying main topics

Objective of lesson: Students will identify main topics of informational texts

Common Core State Standard used: RI.2.2: Identify the main topic of a multi-paragraph text as well as the focus of specific paragraphs within the text.

Materials needed:

Choice of informational text (samples included)

Post-its or Writing paper

Time for lesson: 30-45 minutes

Lesson:

- Share the passage(s) with students. Explain that writing has one topic that is related to every sentence in the paragraph and whole passage. This topic is usually mentioned in the first or second sentence of a paragraph.
- As students read each passage have them mark or write the main topic using only one word. (This is great to use with single paragraphs as a quick review)

Assessment: Grading should be based on marking the appropriate main topic(s).

Sample Paragraphs:

We can watch things around us move. When something is in motion, it changes its position. Objects can move from one place to another. They can move in many directions. If you roll a ball, it might move in a straight line, or it might move in a curve. A swing can move back and forth. A light switch can move up and down. Fans have blades that move in a circle. (Topic: Motion)

Gravity is a force that makes all objects be attracted to each other. The bigger the object is, the more it attracts things. Since nothing on Earth is bigger than planet Earth itself, all the things (and people) on Earth are attracted by Earth. Everything is pulled toward the center of the planet, which is why things fall to the ground. It is also why people and things stay on the ground instead of floating around. Earth is even large enough to attract our moon. That's why we can always see it in our sky! (Topic: Gravity)

Even professional writers do not write everything perfectly the first time. They have to revise their work. When you revise your writing, you look for ways to change it that will make it better. You check your spelling, and you make sure that you have used capitals, periods, and other punctuation marks in the best way. You look for words that can be taken out or traded for different, more exciting words. You make sure that your words help the reader get a picture in his mind when he reads them. (Topic: Revising)

RI 2.3 Lesson One

Title: How Do I...

Topic: Describing the steps of a process

Objective of lesson: Students will describe and demonstrate the steps of a given process.

Common Core State Standard used: RI.2.3: Describe the connection between a series of historical events, scientific ideas or concepts, or steps in technical procedures in a text.

Materials needed:

Actual or toy materials to create a sandwich

Time for lesson: 50-60 minutes

Lesson: (Large group or small groups)

- Tell students that you are going to use your imagination today. You are going to pretend that you are an alien from another planet and you are visiting earth. Explain that though you understand English, you do not know how to do basic tasks. Tell them you want to make a (whatever) sandwich.
- Have students explain to you how to make a sandwich. Make sure that they tell you to open the refrigerator if using cold cuts or how to hold the knife if spreading mustard or any other item.
- Allow students to take turns saying one or two steps. To create a real challenge, if students do not tell you how to properly hold a

knife, pick it up incorrectly and try to use it. *This activity can get messy, but is lots of fun*

- Follow up with students - Have students write a short informational piece on "How to Make a Bed."

Assessment: Grading should be based on participation and explanations and the follow up activity.

RI 2.3 Lesson Two

Title: Line Up

Topic: Ordering the steps of a process

Objective of lesson: Students will order the steps in a process to create a line of events

Common Core State Standard used: RI.2.3: Describe the connection between a series of historical events, scientific ideas or concepts, or steps in technical procedures in a text.

Materials needed:

Large rectangular blocks

Erasable labels for the blocks (dry erase tags work well)

Passages about processes

Time for lesson: 30-40 minutes

Lesson: (Small groups)

- Tell students you are going to read them a paragraph about a process, such as building a bridge or doing a science experiment.
- Next have students list the steps of the process described
- Write each step on a block
- Mix up the blocks
- Now have students work together to line them up with several inches between each

- If the blocks are in order, tap the first one and watch the domino effect. Now remove a step and ask students what will happen (It will not fall correctly). This is why doing things in order is best, so things fall into place smoothly.

Assessment: Grading should be based on participation, ordering, and identifying steps in a process.

RI 2.4 Lesson One

Title: Say What?

Topic: Identify the meaning of unknown words

Objective of lesson: Students will identify possible meanings for unknown words using context clues.

Common Core State Standard used: RI.2.4: Determine the meaning of words and phrases in a text relevant to a *grade 2 topic or subject area.*

Materials needed:

Sentences with unfamiliar words (Worksheet included)

Time for lesson: 20-30 minutes

Lesson: (Small groups)

- Tell students that you are going to read sentences or short paragraphs that will have an unfamiliar word in it. Explain that you will read the passage twice if needed.
- After readings have students decide what the word must mean in context as well as explain why they believe this. Ask other students if they agree with the definition.

Assessment: Grading should be based on correct answers and participation

Sample Sentences

1) The class got extra recess for being well behaved, they were ecstatic. (excited)

2) Most children abhor (hate, dislike) eating broccoli.

3) The dog bounded (leaped, ran) across the large open field.

4) The house had not been cleaned in several weeks, it was sullied. (dirty, unclean, filthy)

5) The crowd was hushed (quiet) as they waited for the player to shoot the basket at the last minute.

6) The car accelerated (sped up, moved faster) as the driver stepped on the gas pedal.

7) My mother was furious (angry, mad) when I broke her favorite vase.

8) I scaled (climbed) the ladder to reach the top of the slide.

9) I tumbled (fell) to the ground when my shoe broke.

10) I dashed (ran) across the room to answer the phone.

RI 2.4 Lesson Two

Title: Word-Picture Match

Topic: Identify the meaning of unknown words through the use of illustrations

Objective of lesson: Students will identify possible meanings for unknown words using context clues.

Common Core State Standard used: RI.2.4: Determine the meaning of words and phrases in a text relevant to a *grade 2 topic or subject area.*

Materials needed:

Sentences with unfamiliar words (Samples included)

Picture pairs to accompany new words

Time for lesson: 30-45 minutes

Lesson: (Pairs)

- Explain to students if an unfamiliar word shows up in a sentence of passage, pictures can often help us figure out what the word means.
- Tell students you are going to allow them to work in pairs to match sentences with the pictures that show the true meaning of the sentence. Then students can share their thoughts with the class.

Assessment: Grading should be based on correct answers and participation in pairs.

Samples:

1) I scaled the slide, all the way to the top.

2) I plunged into the water.

3) The luggage was placed on the plane.

4) The look on her face was miserable.

RI 2.5 Lesson One

Title: I Know This Is Important

Topic: Identification of text features

Objective of lesson: Students will locate important words in a passage by recognizing bold or italicized print.

Common Core State Standard used: RI.2.5: Know and use various text features (e.g., captions, bold print, subheadings, glossaries, indexes, electronic menus, icons) to locate key facts or information in a text efficiently.

Materials needed:

Text (textbooks) that contain italicized and bold terms

Mini dry-erase boards

Dry-erase markers

Time for lesson: 40-50 minutes

Lesson:

- Explain to students that when we read textbooks there are certain features that help the reader know what is important. One thing is **bold** writing, which is darker writing. Another is *italics* which makes the writing look kind of wavy.
- Assign students to work in pairs and then assign each group one or two pages of a book.

- Have students search the pages and look for important words that are located there. They can write each word down on the dry erase board and mark them as b for bold or i for italics. Have students share their findings with another group and then with the class.

Assessment: Grading should be based on recognition and recording of these terms as well as labeling.

RI 2.5 Lesson Two

Title: Finding What's Important

Topic: Identification of text features

Objective of lesson: Students will locate important words in a passage by recognizing bold or italicized print.

Common Core State Standard used: RI.2.5: Know and use various text features (e.g., captions, bold print, subheadings, glossaries, indexes, electronic menus, icons) to locate key facts or information in a text efficiently.

Materials needed:

Sample Page

Pencils

Highlighters

Time for lesson: 40-50 minutes

Lesson:

- Explain to students that when we read textbooks there are certain features that help the reader know what is important. Some things that are important include captions, which are under pictures, bold print, italics, and subheadings which help break apart a chapter.
- Give each child or pair of children a sample page (included).

- Allow students to label and highlight all subheadings, bold, italics, and captions.

Assessment: Grading should be based on recognition as well as labeling terms correctly.

Sample Page:

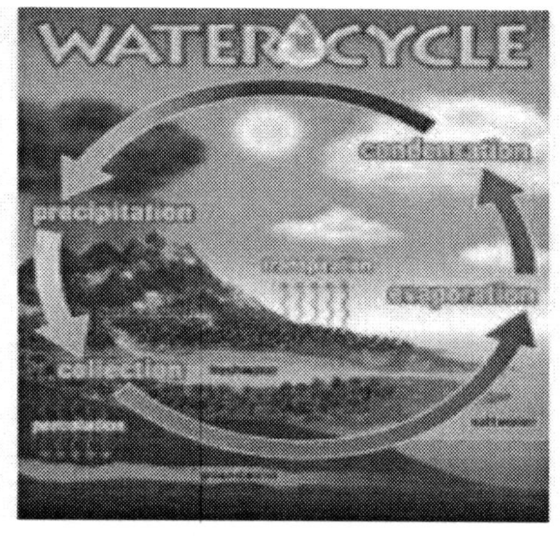

This picture shows the water cycle and all of the steps involved

Water Cycle

Four Steps in a Cycle

When you look around the Earth at all the oceans, seas, and rivers, when you consider all the rain, snow, and sleet, it seems like water on this planet is limitless. The fact is, though, there is a limited amount of water. To learn more about this science, keep reading.

Evaporation:

Since we are talking about a cycle, there really is no beginning we can start from, so let's just start at evaporation. A good way to think about evaporation is to consider how many puddles there are after a storm. Especially on a hot day, when the sun comes out after a storm, many puddles disappear quickly. It doesn't actually disappear, though, it just changes form, from liquid to water vapor. This process actually removes heat from the environment, which is why sweat evaporating from your body cools you off. Changing from a liquid to a gas, water then travels up through the atmosphere, eventually changing back into a liquid through another process in the water cycle.

Condensation:

So now that our water has evaporated up out of the puddle, lake, stream, etc., what happens to it? Does it just keep going up and up and into outer space? Well, if you've ever seen rain you know that it comes back down to us, but how does it turn back into liquid water? Condensation is the process by which the water vapor from our evaporation section becomes liquid again.

Precipitation

Since condensation is the reformation of water vapor, what makes that water fall back down to Earth? Even though clouds are made of condensed water, the droplets are so small they are less dense than the air beneath them, meaning they weigh too little to fall. These droplets are so small, in fact, that it takes millions of them just to form a drop of water which weighs enough to fall. When enough of these drops form, they all fall in the form of rain, snow, hail, and sleet. Even though precipitation requires a few complicated processes to occur, over 121 trillion gallons of precipitation falls every year.

Collection

Now that water has fallen, all it has to do is be evaporated again, right? Well, partly. Eventually, the water will evaporate again. In fact, if we just look at the puddles from earlier, the water collected there will evaporate rather quickly after the precipitation stops falling. But the keyword in the last sentence was collected. The water needs to be collected, even if only for a short time, before it can evaporate again.

Water is collected in a few different ways. The most obvious and direct way is when water falls into water. In this case, the precipitation becomes part of that water supply and will over the course of time become vapor again. Water can also fall to Earth and become part of the "ground water." This type of water is used by plants and can also run over the earth and make its way to water sources.

RI 2.6 Lesson One

Title: This Is About

Topic: Identification of the main purpose of text

Objective of lesson: Students will identify the main purpose of a short passage.

Common Core State Standard used: RI.2.6: Identify the main purpose of a text, including what the author wants to answer, explain, or describe.

Materials needed:

Passages (Samples included)

Dry erase markers

Mini dry erase boards

Time for lesson: 35-45 minutes

Lesson:

- Explain to students that sometimes when we are reading, we must read an entire passage before we understand what the author is talking about or trying to answer. This is because the author is not always direct. Tell students you are going to practice trying to figure out what the author is talking about in a few short passages.

- Have students listen to a passage and when they know what it is about write it down on the dry erase board. When you have finished reading the passage, have students hold up their answer.

Assessment: Grading should be based on correct answers and participation.

Sample passages:

Many people think they cannot fly, but these fowl can. However, they can only fly very short distances. They create eggs in different colors, but mostly white and brown. Both the bird and the eggs can be eaten. (Chickens)

These vehicles are some of the fastest around. They are usually scene on a racetrack travelling at over 100 miles per hour. Some have sponsors so they are painted different colors and have different numbers. (Racecar)

Tasty, crunchy, and salty, these are a favorite snack of many people in America. These treats come in all flavors, but all start out as potatoes that are harvested from the ground. What is your favorite flavor combination? Mine is cheddar and sour cream. (Potato chips)

You know what is weird? My favorite drink comes from an animal. Once it has been pasteurized, made safe for drinking, it has to stay in the refrigerator. If I am really lucky I can add strawberry or chocolate syrup and make it extra special. I bet many people will have my favorite drink for lunch today. (Milk)

RI 2.6 Lesson Two

Title: Understanding a Textbook

Topic: Identification of the main purpose of text

Objective of lesson: Students will identify the main purpose of passages in a textbook

Common Core State Standard used: RI.2.6: Identify the main purpose of a text, including what the author wants to answer, explain, or describe.

Materials needed:

Textbooks

Time for lesson: 30-45 minutes

Lesson:

- Explain to students that you are going to use a textbook to learn about author's purpose because textbooks offer lots of hints.
- Have students open to the beginning of a chapter. Show students the title and any subheadings. Explain that a chapter title tells what the chapter will be about overall and the subheadings hint at particular sections.
- Have students read a few chapter titles and discuss as a large group. Next have students try several on their own, give page numbers with subheadings and have students try to determine main topics for those sections.

Assessment: Grading should be based on correct answers and participation.

RI 2.7 Lesson One

Title: Show Me With A Diagram

Topic: Using diagrams to make information easier to understand

Objective of lesson: Students will create a diagram to show the steps of a process

Common Core State Standard used: RI.2.7: Explain how specific images (e.g., a diagram showing how a machine works) contribute to and clarify a text.

Materials needed:

Paper

Crayons

Passage (Sample included)

Time for lesson: 50-60 minutes

Lesson:

- Explain to students that pictures sometimes help us understand what is happening in a passage. In the same way, charts and diagrams help us understand how something works.
- Have students read the passage and create a diagram or picture with labels to show what is being described.

Assessment: Grading should be based on correct labeling and a drawing that is applicable. Then have students create their own.

Sample Passage:

Brushing your teeth is very important, but very young children do not always know what to do. So you must remember to teach them that only a small amount of toothpaste goes onto the toothbrush bristles. Putting toothpaste all over the toothbrush would be messy. The toothpaste comes in a labeled container. There are many types and flavors available. Once toothpaste is on the toothbrush, one should run just a little water over the toothpaste. Next, you should put the toothbrush in your mouth and start brushing your teeth. One way to remember how to brush is to remember the rhyme "Up like a rocket, down like the rain, back and forth like a choo-choo train." Make sure to brush all your teeth, front and back. Next, rinse off the toothbrush and brush with just water to get all the toothpaste off of your teeth. Make sure you do not swallow toothpaste, it can make you sick. Finally, if you need to, rinse your mouth with a little water in a cup and spit out the water. Clean off your toothbrush with water and place it in a clean place. The actual brushing should take at least two minutes.

Sample diagram:

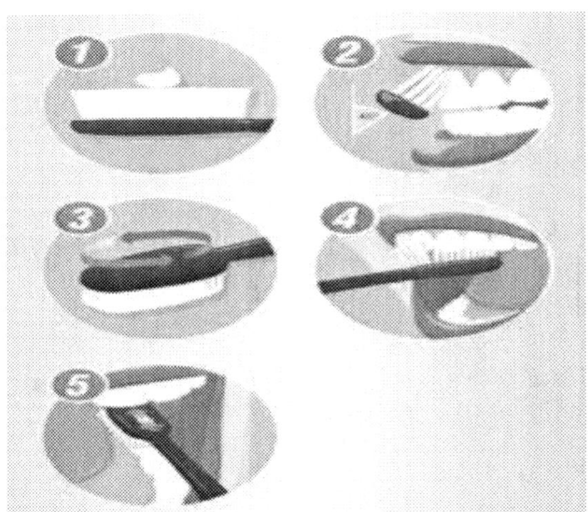

RI 2.7 Lesson Two

Title: Why?

Topic: Explaining diagram usefulness

Objective of lesson: Students will write an explanation of why a diagram is helpful by citing at least three reasons it is of help.

Common Core State Standard used: RI.2.7: Explain how specific images (e.g., a diagram showing how a machine works) contribute to and clarify a text.

Materials needed:

Paper

Pencil

Passage with diagram/Same passage without

Time for lesson: 35-45 minutes

Lesson:

- Explain to students that pictures sometimes help us understand what is happening in a passage. In the same way, charts and diagrams help us understand how something works.
- Have students read the passage without a diagram. Ask students if they completely understand everything that they read.
- Now have students read the same passage with a diagram. Does the diagram help you understand?

- Have students list at least three reasons that diagrams may help understanding.

Assessment: Grading should be based on participation and three valid reasons for furthering understanding.

RI 2.8 Lesson One

Title: Sort It Out

Topic: Supporting details

Objective of lesson: Students will separate supporting details into categories.

Common Core State Standard used: RI.2.8: Describe how reasons support specific points the author makes in a text.

Materials needed:

Worksheet (Included)

Glue

Time for lesson: 40-50 minutes

Lesson:

- Explain to students that when we read there is always a main topic followed by several statements that support or explain that main topic. Give an example from a text book.
- Tell students that they are going to do some sorting. There are two main topics and several supporting details listed. Cut apart the details and place them under the correct main topic.

Assessment: Grading should be based on correct placement.

Living Items	Nonliving Items

Breathes air	Requires food or energy
Never dies	Can reproduce
Cannot reproduce	Needs water
Trees	Rocks
Money	Flowers

RI 2.8 Lesson Two

Title: The Proof Is InThe Details

Topic: Creating supporting details

Objective of lesson: Students will write details on a given topic

Common Core State Standard used: RI.2.8: Describe how reasons support specific points the author makes in a text.

Materials needed:

Topics (Sample included)

Pencil

Paper

Time for lesson: 40-50 minutes

Lesson:

- Explain to students that details make the writing and just as you try to make points to win an argument, details support a point in a story.
- Give students a list of topics and allow them to pick two or three. Have them write at least three supporting details/arguments for each main topic. When they are finished they can share with the class.

Assessment: Grading should be based on having strong supporting details.

Sample Topics:

1) Chocolate ice cream is better than any other type of sweet.

2) Water is important for all things that are living.

3) Soccer is much more fun than football.

4) A dead plant can still be classified as a living unit.

5) Cooking can be fun.

6) Math is a tough subject.

7) Gym class is fun.

8) Television can be educational.

9) Staying clean is important.

10) Dogs make better pets than cats.

RI 2.9 Lesson One

Title: What's Different?

Topic: Finding differences

Objective of lesson: Students will spot differences in illustrations

Common Core State Standard used: RI.2.9: Compare and contrast the most important points presented by two texts on the same topic.

Materials needed:

Similar pictures (Samples included)

Time for lesson: 15-20 minutes

Lesson:

- Explain to students that sometimes even factual information will offer different points of view. Both sets of information may be true, but only certain facts are shared. Explain that to be a good reader we must be able to spot differences quickly and then review to see which information is most important.
- Tell students they are going to do a fun, yet quick skill builder to be able to spot difference. Hand out the sample pictures.

Assessment: Grading should be based on finding all the differences

Sample Pictures: Find the differences

RI 2.9 Lesson Two

Title: Spot The Change

Topic: Finding differences in text

Objective of lesson: Students will spot simple differences in text

Common Core State Standard used: RI.2.9: Compare and contrast the most important points presented by two texts on the same topic.

Materials needed:

Similar sentences (Samples included)

Mini dry erase boards

Dry-erase markers

Time for lesson: 25-30 minutes

Lesson:

- Explain to students that sometimes even factual information will offer different points of view. Both sets of information may be true, but only certain facts are shared. Explain that to be a good reader we must be able to spot differences quickly and then review to see which information is most important.
- Tell students they are going to listen to sets of sentences, two in each set. The sentences will have one difference, usually one word. Once they hear the different word the students should write the pair of differing words on the dry erase board and wait for the teacher to check the answer.

Assessment: Grading should be based on correct answers and listening skills.

Sample Sentence Sets

1) The light turned green suddenly.

The light turned red suddenly.

2) The dog barked at the little girl on the bike.

The dog growled at the little girl on the bike.

3) The kitten scratched at the chair.

The kitten scratched at the sofa.

4) His foot was broken when he fell off the large rock.

His foot was injured when he fell off the large rock.

5) The blue van slowed down at the stop sign.

The green van stopped at the stop sign.

RF 2.3 Lesson One

Title: The Long And Short Of It

Topic: Long and short vowels

Objective of lesson: Students will recognize words with short and long vowel sounds.

Common Core State Standard used: RF.2.3: Know and apply grade-level phonics and word analysis skills in decoding words.

- CCSS.ELA-Literacy.RF.2.3a Distinguish long and short vowels when reading regularly spelled one-syllable words.
- CCSS.ELA-Literacy.RF.2.3b Know spelling-sound correspondences for additional common vowel teams.
- CCSS.ELA-Literacy.RF.2.3c Decode regularly spelled two-syllable words with long vowels.
- CCSS.ELA-Literacy.RF.2.3d Decode words with common prefixes and suffixes.
- CCSS.ELA-Literacy.RF.2.3e Identify words with inconsistent but common spelling-sound correspondences.
- CCSS.ELA-Literacy.RF.2.3f Recognize and read grade-appropriate irregularly spelled words.

Materials needed:

Glue

Sorting words (Included)

Scissors

Time for lesson: 30-45 minutes

Lesson:

- Remind students of the sounds short and long vowels make when used in words. Explain that knowing the sounds of different vowel combinations help us read correctly, even when unfamiliar words come up.
- Offer the following example: What does dote say? Now what does dot say? The first is a long vowel and the second a short vowel.
- Explain that the students will get a list of words, some will have long vowels and some will have short. They are to sort the words and glue them under the right heading.

Assessment: Grading should be based on correct placement of long and short vowel words.

Long **Short**

Soda	Pop
Cob	Cone
Cane	Can
Sew	Show
Turn	Dog
Tune	Dare
Dark	Line
Heat	Hedge

RF 2.3 Lesson Two

Title: Break The Code

Topic: Decoding words with prefixes and suffixes

Objective of lesson: Students will decode words with prefixes and suffixes

Common Core State Standard used: RF.2.3: Know and apply grade-level phonics and word analysis skills in decoding words.

- CCSS.ELA-Literacy.RF.2.3a Distinguish long and short vowels when reading regularly spelled one-syllable words.
- CCSS.ELA-Literacy.RF.2.3b Know spelling-sound correspondences for additional common vowel teams.
- CCSS.ELA-Literacy.RF.2.3c Decode regularly spelled two-syllable words with long vowels.
- CCSS.ELA-Literacy.RF.2.3d Decode words with common prefixes and suffixes.
- CCSS.ELA-Literacy.RF.2.3e Identify words with inconsistent but common spelling-sound correspondences.
- CCSS.ELA-Literacy.RF.2.3f Recognize and read grade-appropriate irregularly spelled words.

Materials needed:

Pencils

Worksheet (Include)

Time for lesson: 45-50 minutes

Lesson:

- Explain to students that prefixes and suffixes can change the meaning of a word. Use the example school, school is where you are now or what you attend to learn, but add the prefix preschool and it means before school, so before you are old enough for regular school you go to preschool.
- Tell students they are going to do a simple worksheet to practice decoding words with prefixes and suffixes. These words will have a prefix, a suffix, or both and the meaning must be determined.

Assessment: Grading should be based on correct word decoding

Sample Worksheet:

Pre - before	Ab - away from	Un - not	Mega-great	Multi- many
Ed - past tense	Ness- state of being	En - to become	Able - ability	

Sample: Abnormal means Away from normal

1) Preterm means ______________________________

2) Untie means ______________________________

3) Cried means ______________________________

4) Megaphone means ___________________________

5) Moveable means ____________________________

6) Lengthen means ____________________________

7) Messiness means ___________________________

8) Cleanliness means __________________________

9) Multi-tool means ___________________________

10) Drinkable means ___________________________

RF 2.4 Lesson One

Title: Sounds Like

Topic: Fluency building through homophones

Objective of lesson: Students will build fluency by practicing homophones

Common Core State Standard used: RF.2.4: Read with sufficient accuracy and fluency to support comprehension.

- CCSS.ELA-Literacy.RF.2.4a Read grade-level text with purpose and understanding.
- CCSS.ELA-Literacy.RF.2.4b Read grade-level text orally with accuracy, appropriate rate, and expression.
- CCSS.ELA-Literacy.RF.2.4c Use context to confirm or self-correct word recognition and understanding, rereading as necessary.

Materials needed:

List of homophones

Time for lesson: 5 minutes (per child)

Lesson:

- Present students one at a time with the list of homophones and have them read aloud while being timed. Record the time each day to build fluency. Correct any reading errors.

Assessment: Grading should be based on word accuracy and shortened time to read.

Homophones:

Blue	Blew	Red	Read	Ad
Ate	Eight	Band	Banned	Bare
Bear	Buy	By	Bye	To
Too	Two	Bail	Bail	Beat

RF 2.4 Lesson Two

Title: Fluency Bingo

Topic: Fluency building through Bingo

Objective of lesson: Students will build fluency by recognizing common sight words

Common Core State Standard used: RF.2.4: Read with sufficient accuracy and fluency to support comprehension.

- CCSS.ELA-Literacy.RF.2.4a Read grade-level text with purpose and understanding.
- CCSS.ELA-Literacy.RF.2.4b Read grade-level text orally with accuracy, appropriate rate, and expression.
- CCSS.ELA-Literacy.RF.2.4c Use context to confirm or self-correct word recognition and understanding, rereading as necessary.

Materials needed:

Bingo cards (Template included)

Sight words list (http://tarpey.cusd.com/documents/2ndSightWords.pdf)

Bingo markers or highlighters

Time for lesson: 5-30 minutes (per game)

Lesson:

- Give students a blank Bingo card
- Display a list of sight words for students to choose from for the card
- Have students place one word in each square (There will be leftover words
- At random choose words until a child has Bingo
- Have students read out words for Bingo to check for accuracy

Assessment: Grading should be based on participation and correct reading of winning words.

B	I	N	G	O
		Free Space		

W 2.1 Lesson One

Title: Stop In The Name Of Writing

Topic: Writing and supporting opinions

Objective of lesson: Students will create an opinion piece about a story.

Common Core State Standard used: W.2.1: Write opinion pieces in which they introduce the topic or book they are writing about, state an opinion, supply reasons that support the opinion, use linking words (e.g.,*because, and, also*) to connect opinion and reasons, and provide a concluding statement or section.

Materials needed:

Crayons (Red, yellow, green)

Time for lesson: 40-50 minutes

Lesson:

- Explain to students that they are going to write a brief story to explain an opinion. Tell them an opinion is something like 'Yellow is the prettiest color ever'. If you are going to say something like that then you should be able to back it up with comments about why you think yellow is the prettiest color.
- Show students the stoplight method for writing. The green section, the first one is where the opinion is stated. The next section, yellow, means to slow down and explain the opinion with supporting feelings and thoughts while using transition words

such as next, because, and also. The final section is red and wraps up the writing with a final statement. It may take practice before students can do this alone, so working as a large group at first may be best.

- Have students write a statement about their favorite food and underline it in green on the paper. This is the opening statement. 'Pizza is my favorite food.'
- Now have students write one reason why this is their favorite food. 'Pizza is my favorite because I like melted cheese.' Have students write a second statement with a transition word. 'Pizza also has lots of toppings to choose from.' Both statements should be underlined in yellow.
- The final statement should wrap things up 'That is why pizza is my favorite food.' This should be underlined in red.

Assessment: Grading should be based on writing accuracy and the use of appropriate opinions as well as grammatical correctness.

W 2.1 Lesson Two

Title: Make Your Point

Topic: Writing and supporting opinions

Objective of lesson: Students will create an opinion piece about a story.

Common Core State Standard used: W.2.1: Write opinion pieces in which they introduce the topic or book they are writing about, state an opinion, supply reasons that support the opinion, use linking words (e.g.,*because, and, also*) to connect opinion and reasons, and provide a concluding statement or section.

Materials needed:

Graphic organizer (Included)

Time for lesson: 30-45 minutes

Lesson:

- Explain to students that everyone has opinions. Opinions are statements that are not true for everyone. Something such as the best flavor of ice cream is strawberry. While I may feel that way, someone else may like chocolate better.
- Sometimes we try to convince others our opinion is best or why we believe such an opinion. This is called supporting an opinion. Tell students they are going to come up with an opinion about (your choice of topics).

- Next have students write that opinion in the point of the exclamation point. Next have students write at least three statements supporting that opinion in the main part of the point.

Assessment: Grading should be based on writing an actual opinion and supporting it with realistic reasons.

W 2.2 Lesson One

Title: Just The Facts Please

Topic: Writing with supporting ideas

Objective of lesson: Students will create a written piece that uses facts to back up the initial statement

Common Core State Standard used: W.2.2: Write informative/explanatory texts in which they introduce a topic, use facts and definitions to develop points, and provide a concluding statement or section.

Materials needed:

Text book (or informational texts)

Graphic organizer or paper (sample included)

Time for lesson: 45-60 minutes

Lesson:

- Give students a fact or allow them to find a factual statement in a textbook. Remind students that facts are things that are true for everyone, such as 'A tree is a living unit' or 'The sun is very hot'.
- Next explain to students that they are going to find more information to back up this statement. Assigning a particular chapter or page numbers to use to find facts is best when starting out, but allowing students to find books later on builds skill. Students can work with a partner or small group.

- Have students write out their fact and three supporting statements in list form.

Assessment: Grading should be based on writing an actual fact or statement and supporting it with realistic reasons from books or online.

W 2.2 Lesson Two

Title: Book Report

Topic: Writing with supporting ideas

Objective of lesson: Students will create a written piece that uses facts to back up the initial statement

Common Core State Standard used: W.2.2: Write informative/explanatory texts in which they introduce a topic, use facts and definitions to develop points, and provide a concluding statement or section.

Materials needed:

Access to a library

Writing paper

Construction paper

Markers

Time for lesson: 30-40 sessions for several days

Lesson:

- Have students choose a topic that interests them, something such as a specific type of animal, or how something is made.
- Take students to the library to find one or two books about their chosen topic.

- Have students review the topic and read their books. As they read have them write out several (3-5) facts about their topic.
- Next help students to write a topic sentence to introduce their topic. This may need to be completed in small groups so a strong sentence is created.
- Next allow children to write their facts after the topic sentence, encourage the use of transition words.
- Finally, have students write a concluding sentence. To make the report extra special, have students decorate a cover and choose a title.

Assessment: Grading should be based on writing an actual fact or statement and supporting it with realistic reasons from books or online, writing and grammar can also be considered.

W 2.3 Lesson One

Title: Pudding Pie

Topic: Writing a narrative about a recently viewed process

Objective of lesson: Students will write a brief summary of an activity that has been demonstrated

Common Core State Standard used: W.2.3: Write narratives in which they recount a well-elaborated event or short sequence of events, include details to describe actions, thoughts, and feelings, use temporal words to signal event order, and provide a sense of closure.

Materials needed:

Instant pudding mix (including ingredients to complete)

Mini Fila shells (no cooking required)

Paper (Graphic organizer included)

Pencil

Time for lesson: 30-45 minutes

Lesson:

- Explain to students that you are going to make a tasty treat. Tell them that even though they will get to taste the treat, they must pay very close attention to the details because they will be writing about it afterward.
- Make pudding according to the box specifications. Be very vocal and overly explanatory as to each step and the amount of

ingredients. (Always check for allergies before cooking in a classroom)

- After the pudding is made remove the mini shells and put a single spoonful of pudding in each. Allow children to taste if desired.
- After the taste test tell students that they will use the recipe card to write about what they viewed. Tell them to be very specific and include as many details, in order, as they can remember.

Assessment: Grading should be based on appropriate writing and having at least five detailed steps (more if desired).

Recipe: ______________________________

From the Kitchen of: ______________________________

W 2.3 Lesson Two

Title: One Time At…

Topic: Writing a narrative about a personal event

Objective of lesson: Students will write a brief summary of an activity that has been demonstrated

Common Core State Standard used: W.2.3: Write narratives in which they recount a well-elaborated event or short sequence of events, include details to describe actions, thoughts, and feelings, use temporal words to signal event order, and provide a sense of closure.

Materials needed:

Paper

Pencil

Time for lesson: 45-60 minutes

Lesson:

- Tell students that they are going to write a story about something they have done that was enjoyable
- Allow time for students to write a narrative and draw a picture if time permits.
- Have students read stories aloud to small groups or the class as a show and tell.

Assessment: Grading should be based on appropriate writing and having at least five detailed steps (more if desired).

W 2.5 Lesson One

Title: Working Together

Topic: Editing

Objective of lesson: Students will work together to edit papers

Common Core State Standard used: W.2.5: With guidance and support from adults and peers, focus on a topic and strengthen writing as needed by revising and editing.

Materials needed:

Highlighters

List of editing/partner work (Sample included)

Time for lesson: 30-40 minutes

Lesson:

- Explain to students that one way to become a better writer is to help each other.
- Review the rules for helping others edit a paper.
- Allow students to edit one another's paper during an assignment.

Assessment: Grading should be based on appropriate revisions and ability to work together.

Editing Together

1) Be positive, find the good to comment on as well as correcting errors

2) Ask questions, if something is unclear, ask the writer what it means

3) Be open, not everything you read will be something enjoyable, but be nice anyway

4) Edit honestly, mark spelling and grammar areas and make suggestions

5) Accept help, no one is perfect, ask and accept help to become better at what you do.

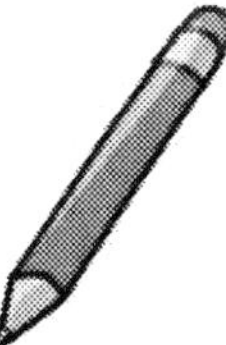

W 2.5 Lesson Two

Title: Clean It Up

Topic: Editing

Objective of lesson: Students will edit basic errors in writing

Common Core State Standard used: W.2.5: With guidance and support from adults and peers, focus on a topic and strengthen writing as needed by revising and editing.

Materials needed:

Highlighters

Worksheet (Samples)

Time for lesson: 15-20 minutes

Lesson: (Great for early morning work before class officially starts)

- Hand out only three to five sentences a day and have students mark the errors and rewrite sentences correctly.
- First several times you use this lesson, check as a whole group. After students have a better understanding, grade independently.

Assessment: Grading should be based on appropriate revisions as well as correct mark-ups.

Sample Corrections:

Correct the following sentences and then rewrite.

1) At thre oclock the bell will ring to dismiss the class?

____

2) "I wood luv to go to the movies, she said when axed.

____

3) the kitten fell off the sofa shortly aftr fallin asleep?

____

4) Where did the for squirrels in the yard run too when you open the door.

____

5) The childrens toys were placed in shelves neatly at the end of each day!

____

W 2.6 Lesson One

Title: Create A Laugh

Topic: Using technology to write and share

Objective of lesson: Students will create a unique comic strip with captions using the Internet

Common Core State Standard used: W.2.6: With guidance and support from adults, use a variety of digital tools to produce and publish writing, including in collaboration with peers.

Materials needed:

Computers w/Internet

Website: http://www.readwritethink.org/parent-afterschool-resources/games-tools/comic-creator-a-30237.html

Time for lesson: 10-20 minutes - per small group

Lesson:

- Use during small group time.
- Tell students that they are going to use the computer to create a comic strip like what can be found in the paper.
- Help students log into the computer and the site listed above.

- Students will have to enter the title of their comic strip as well as their name. (Information, including comic strips are not saved after being created)
- Have students choose at least three panels in which to add characters.
- Allow students to choose backgrounds, characters, and extras. Have students write their captions in the small box below the frame.
- Have students print the comic to display and to complete grading.

Assessment: Grading should be based on appropriate use of the computer as well as an understandable comic strip.

W 2.6 Lesson Two

Title: Building A Story

Topic: Using technology to enhance collaborative writing

Objective of lesson: Students will create a group story using a white board

Common Core State Standard used: W.2.6: With guidance and support from adults, use a variety of digital tools to produce and publish writing, including in collaboration with peers.

Materials needed:

White board w/pen

Time for lesson: 10-15 minutes - per small group

Lesson: (Small groups of 4 or 5 work best)

- Students should be taught to use the whiteboard appropriately before completing this type of work.
- Offer students a story starter that you write on the white board.
- One at a time, have students add a sentence to the story, until the story is complete.
- Have students copy down the entire story or print if possible.

Assessment: Grading should be based on appropriate input and participation.

W 2.7 Lesson One

Title: Tell Me About It

Topic: Shared research

Objective of lesson: Students will work within a group to share information with the class as a whole.

Common Core State Standard used: W.2.7: Participate in shared research and writing projects (e.g., read a number of books on a single topic to produce a report; record science observations).

Materials needed:

Textbooks for each student or at least two per group

Organizer (Sample included)

Time for lesson: 30-45 minutes

Lesson:

- Assign groups a section of a chapter or passage
- Explain to students that they are going to work in their group to read the passage and then write down three to five main facts that the class needs to know. They will be the teachers today.
- Allow time for group work
- Each group should present what was recorded to the group.

Assessment: Grading should be based on appropriate group work as well as proper reporting to the class.

Sample Organizer:

Names of Group Members ______________________________

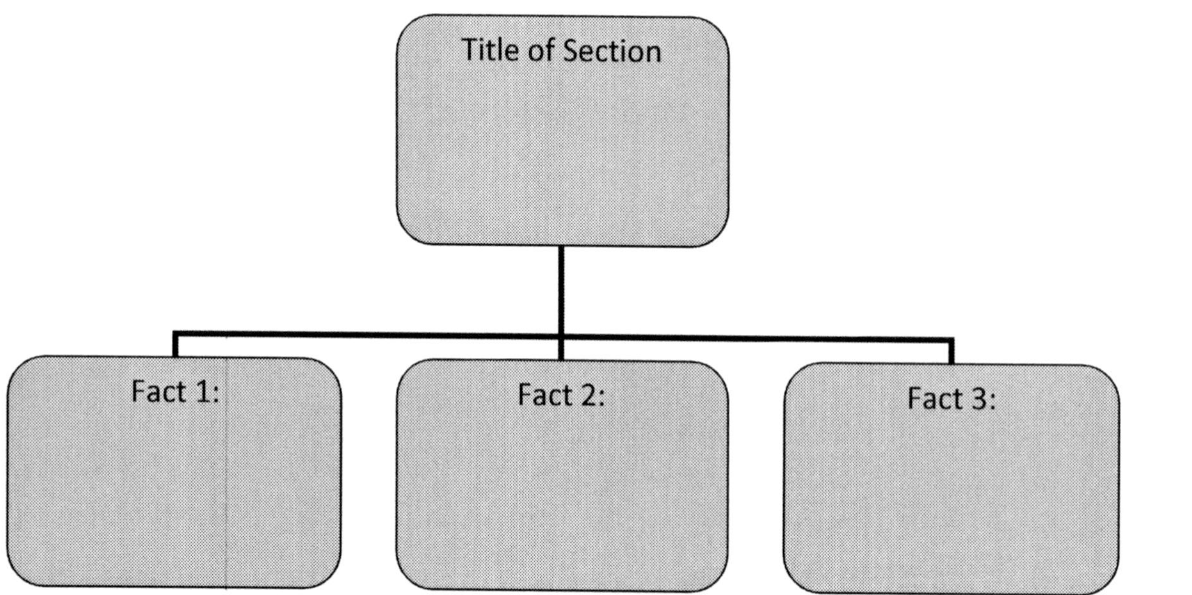

W 2.7 Lesson Two

Title: Around The World

Topic: Shared research

Objective of lesson: Students will work with family members and friends to learn about different places

Common Core State Standard used: W.2.7: Participate in shared research and writing projects (e.g., read a number of books on a single topic to produce a report; record science observations).

Materials needed:

Paper

Pencil

Envelopes

Stamps

Flat Stanley (Included)

Flat Stanley book by Jeff Brown

Time for lesson: 10-30 minutes per session (project can last all year if desired)

Lesson:

- Begin by reading Flat Stanley to set up the project. Tell students you are going to create your own Flat Stanley and they will see what he can learn.

- Have students write or copy letters (sample included) explaining that Flat Stanley wants to learn about all the places he can.
- Place a Flat Stanley with each letter and have students ask parents for addresses of friends and relatives that will participate.
- As letters are received back have students read them and share the photos as well as mark the area on a map.

Assessment: Grading should be based on appropriate writing and participation.

Sample Letter:

Dear Friend,

We hope you are glad to meet Flat Stanley. He is helping us learn. We are trying to learn about different places in the world. We are sending you a special friend to help us learn. Could you please write a little bit about where you live and take a picture of Flat Stanley with you or at your home? Then send the picture and letter back to (address). If you have another friend that would help, could you please send Flat Stanley on and ask them to do the same? Thank you for your help, we hope to learn about places all over the world.

Flat Stanley (Can be colored and cut out to share)

W 2.8 Lesson One

Title: What Was Said?

Topic: Information recall

Objective of lesson: Students will recall information presented by a guest speaker.

Common Core State Standard used: W.2.8: Recall information from experiences or gather information from provided sources to answer a question.

Materials needed:

Guest speaker

Pencil

Paper (Graphic organizer included)

Time for lesson: 30-60 minutes

Lesson:

- Invite a guest speaker into the classroom (parents are often good at this or a list of approved speakers is typically available from the Board of Education)
- Before the speaker arrives tell students to pay attention and ask questions to gain further information.
- Allow students to listen to the speaker.

- Have students write down at least five things they learned from the presentation.

Assessment: Grading should be based on appropriate listening skills and number of items recalled.

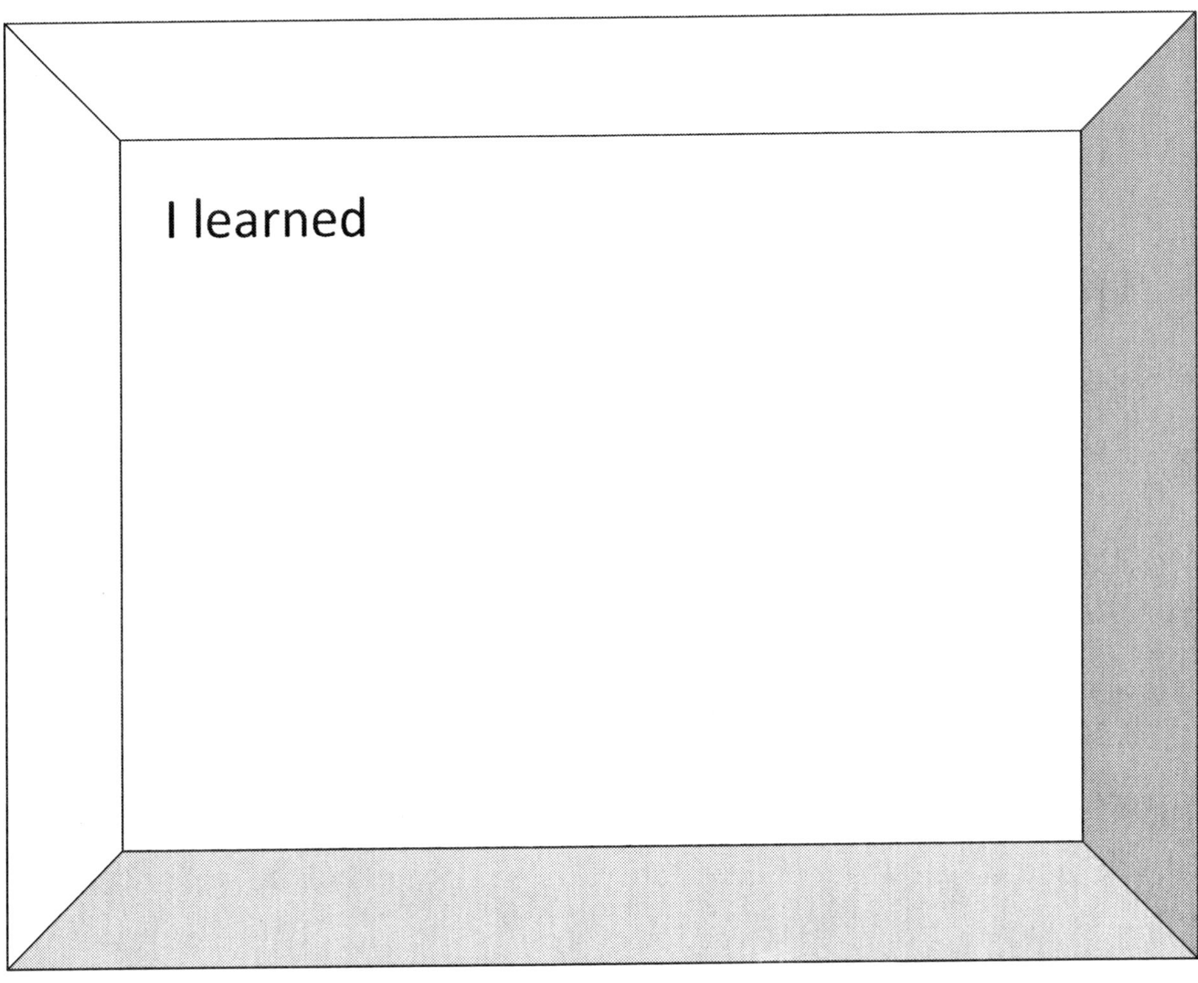

W 2.8 Lesson Two

Title: What's Missing?

Topic: Building Recall

Objective of lesson: Students will recall information

Common Core State Standard used: W.2.8: Recall information from experiences or gather information from provided sources to answer a question.

Materials needed:

Dry erase boards

Dry erase markers

10-20 small objects that can be grouped into smaller groups such as numbers, animals, and plants

Time for lesson: 30-40 minutes

Lesson:

- Place 10-20 objects on a table, do not group the objects. Tell students that they have three minutes to look at the objects and ask what something is if they are unsure.
- Set the timer
- After the students have studied the objects, cover them. Have students write down as many objects as possible that they can remember. Count how many they got correct.

- Next tell students you are going to teach them a trick to remembering more information. This is called grouping. Rearrange the same objects into groups of items (No more than three or four groups).
- Have students erase their boards. Reset the timer for three minutes.
- Cover the objects after three minutes and have students write down how many objects they remember this time. Record the number.

Assessment: Grading should be based on participation.

SL 2.1 Lesson One

Title: Making Rules

Topic: Creating rules for group sharing and talking

Objective of lesson: Students will work together to create a list of rules for working and speaking in groups.

Common Core State Standard used: W.2.1: Participate in collaborative conversations with diverse partners about *grade 2 topics and texts* with peers and adults in small and larger groups.

- CCSS.ELA-Literacy.SL.2.1a Follow agreed-upon rules for discussions (e.g., gaining the floor in respectful ways, listening to others with care, speaking one at a time about the topics and texts under discussion).
- CCSS.ELA-Literacy.SL.2.1b Build on others' talk in conversations by linking their comments to the remarks of others.
- CCSS.ELA-Literacy.SL.2.1c Ask for clarification and further explanation as needed about the topics and texts under discussion.

Materials needed:

Paper

Art supplies

Chart paper

Time for lesson: 30-45 minutes

Lesson:

- Great activity for the beginning of the school year.
- Have students gather in a common area and explain that you need their help to create rules for working in groups and taking turns talking.
- Allow students to share what they think rules should be. Help to reword confusing rules and combine those that can be. The total list should have no more than 4-6 rules. Record on chart paper.
- Next allow students to pick a 'rule' and create a poster to represent that rule. Display posters.

Assessment: Grading should be based on participation and a functional poster.

SL 2.1 Lesson Two

Title: Ice Breakers

Topic: Group sharing following rules

Objective of lesson: Students will share information with one another, and then share to a larger group.

Common Core State Standard used: W.2.1: Participate in collaborative conversations with diverse partners about *grade 2 topics and texts* with peers and adults in small and larger groups.

- CCSS.ELA-Literacy.SL.2.1a Follow agreed-upon rules for discussions (e.g., gaining the floor in respectful ways, listening to others with care, speaking one at a time about the topics and texts under discussion).
- CCSS.ELA-Literacy.SL.2.1b Build on others' talk in conversations by linking their comments to the remarks of others.
- CCSS.ELA-Literacy.SL.2.1c Ask for clarification and further explanation as needed about the topics and texts under discussion.

Materials needed:

Timer

Time for lesson: 30-40 minutes (Depending on group size)

Lesson:

- Explain to students that they are going to practice the rules for sharing in a group and learn a little more about each other.
- Pair students together and tell them they are going to have to take turns answering questions about themselves. They may only answer one question at a time and then they must allow the other person to talk. They will then share the answers of the other person with the class.
- Give students these three questions: What is your whole name? What is your favorite hobby? What is your favorite food?
- Set the timer for 90 seconds and have students try the interaction. After the timer goes off have partners share about each other.

Assessment: Grading should be based on participation and a following the rules of sharing

SL 2.2 Lesson One

Title: Book Club

Topic: Describing details

Objective of lesson: Students will read a book of their choice and share a few details with the class.

Common Core State Standard used: W.2.2: Recount or describe key ideas or details from a text read aloud or information presented orally or through other media.

Materials needed:

Library access

Time for lesson: 60 minutes - presentations

Lesson:

- Have students prepare by visiting the library to get a book to read during the week.
- Set a special time to have students stand in front of the class to share details from their book. If students struggle, ask questions to keep them on track.
- Encourage others to ask questions or make appropriate comments if time permits.

Assessment: Grading should be based on participation and the sharing of relevant information.

SL 2.2 Lesson Two

Title: Then What Happened

Topic: Recounting events

Objective of lesson: Students will recount events in order based on a book

Common Core State Standard used: W.2.2: Recount or describe key ideas or details from a text read aloud or information presented orally or through other media.

Materials needed:

There Was An Old Woman Who Swallowed A Fly by Taback

Time for lesson: 35-45 minutes

Lesson:

- Have students listen to a reading of the book *There Was An Old Woman Who Swallowed A Fly*. Tell them to listen closely as they will be asked to recall the order of the creatures swallowed.
- Have students first list the creatures in order and then draw a picture of each, ending with a picture of the old woman.
- When they finish they can share their thoughts with a partner.

Assessment: Grading should be based on recounting in the correct order.

SL 2.3 Lesson One

Title: Interviewing

Topic: Asking and answering questions

Objective of lesson: Students will ask and answer questions of an important adult in their lives.

Common Core State Standard used: W.2.3: Ask and answer questions about what a speaker says in order to clarify comprehension, gather additional information, or deepen understanding of a topic or issue.

Materials needed:

List of questions (Samples included)

Pencils

Time for lesson: 50-60 minutes

Lesson:

- Tell students that they are going to interview someone, just like reporters on the news. Explain that since this is the first time, they will interview someone they know and have a list of questions already written.
- Work with students to decide on a person they can interview in person or over the phone. A relative such as a grandparent or older neighbor would be ideal.
- Have students interview that person and record their answers.

- In school they can then write a short paragraph about the information that they learned.

Assessment: Grading should be based on interviewing someone as well as recounting the information in a summary.

Sample Questions:

1) Will you tell me what year you were born?

2) What did you do for fun when you were my age?

3) What was your favorite toy?

4) If there something you have done in your life that you are really proud of and will share with me?

SL 2.3 Lesson Two

Title: Jeopardy

Topic: Answering questions

Objective of lesson: Students will answer questions about a recently presented topic

Common Core State Standard used: W.2.3: Ask and answer questions about what a speaker says in order to clarify comprehension, gather additional information, or deepen understanding of a topic or issue.

Materials needed:

Jeopardy questions (Sample board included)

Post-Its

Buzzers or Bells (Raising hands while holding a colored strip of paper also works)

Time for lesson: 25-30 minutes per game

Lesson: (Great test prep)

- Separate students into three teams. Choose a number between one and ten to see which team chooses first. On the board or a wall have five categories related to the topic at hand. Have your questions prepared ahead of time.
- Under each category have five post-its with the numbers 1-5 on them; this is how students will choose a question. As students choose a question read the question you have prepared and

remove that post-it from the board. If the person answering on the team knows the answer they must push their buzzer and be called on. After a question has been answered, all teams move to the next person. Keep score to choose a winner and offer something such as extra credit points if desired.

Assessment: Grading should be based on participation, teamwork, and correct answers.

Sample Board:

Category 1	Category 2	Category 3	Category 4	Category 5
1	1	1	1	1
2	2	2	2	2
3	3	3	3	3
4	4	4	4	4
5	5	5	5	5

SL 2.4 Lesson One

Title: Dinner Time

Topic: Descriptive recounting of previous happenings

Objective of lesson: Students will describe what they had for dinner the night before and add a detailed drawing to help the description.

Common Core State Standard used: W.2.4: Tell a story or recount an experience with appropriate facts and relevant, descriptive details, speaking audibly in coherent sentences.

Materials needed:

Paper

Art supplies

Time for lesson: 60-90 minutes -writing and presenting (2 days)

Lesson:

- Explain to students that they are going to tell the class about something they know a lot about, their dinner the night before.
- Before presenting have students draw a picture of their dinner the night before.
- Next have students hold up their pictures and explain exactly what they had to the class.

Assessment: Grading should be based on drawing and presentation being related.

SL 2.4 Lesson Two

Title: We're Going On A Field Trip

Topic: Recounting events

Objective of lesson: Students will recount the activities and something learned while on a field trip.

Common Core State Standard used: W.2.4: Tell a story or recount an experience with appropriate facts and relevant, descriptive details, speaking audibly in coherent sentences.

Materials needed:

Art supplies

Time for lesson: 40-50 minutes (plus time for field trip)

Lesson:

- After attending a field trip, program, or even an outdoor nature walk have students draw a picture of what they remember most about the event.
- Next have students share aloud with a small or large group about what they found most interesting and what happened during the trip.

Assessment: Grading should be based on coherent, clear speaking ability and the use of clear descriptions.

SL 2.5 Lesson One

Title: Listen To Me

Topic: Recording of self reading

Objective of lesson: Students will use an online recording program to record a book they are reading.

Common Core State Standard used: W.2.5: Create audio recordings of stories or poems; add drawings or other visual displays to stories or recounts of experiences when appropriate to clarify ideas, thoughts, and feelings.

Materials needed:

Computers with free Audacity download
http://audacity.sourceforge.net/

Computer headphones/microphones

Short book or passage of the child's choice

Time for lesson: 10-15 minutes (per child, per computer)

Lesson:

- After showing students how to record their voices online using Audacity, have students record themselves reading a book of their choice.
- Have students listen to their own reading and re-record if desired.

Assessment: Grading should be based on a clear, coherent reading and use of technology.

*Audacity tutorial (made by a child) to review the basics
http://www.youtube.com/watch?v=kTNAZKjTnGA

SL 2.5 Lesson Two

Title: I Wrote A Poem

Topic: Recording of self reading

Objective of lesson: Students will use an online recording program to record a poem they have written

Common Core State Standard used: W.2.5: Create audio recordings of stories or poems; add drawings or other visual displays to stories or recounts of experiences when appropriate to clarify ideas, thoughts, and feelings.

Materials needed:

Computers with free Audacity download http://audacity.sourceforge.net/

Computer headphones/microphones

Paper

Pencil

Time for lesson: 15-30 minutes (per child, per computer)

Lesson:

- Have students choose their favorite color, food, holiday…
- Have students create a short poem (rhyming or non-rhyming) about their choice.

- Next have students find a picture online to represent that color, this will serve as the icon for their poem.
- Have students record themselves reading their poem using Audacity.
- If possible, post poems and readings online on a class page or secure school page (get permission first)

Assessment: Grading should be based on a clear, coherent reading and appropriate use of technology.

SL 2.6 Lesson One

Title: Make It Complete

Topic: Creating complete sentences

Objective of lesson: Students will create unique, complete sentences from segments.

Common Core State Standard used: W.2.6: Produce complete sentences when appropriate to task and situation in order to provide requested detail or clarification.

Materials needed:

Sentence segments (Included)

Time for lesson: 30-45 minutes

Lesson:

- Explain to students that sometimes using only part of a sentence is not appropriate, more information needs to be given.
- Give the following example: Let's pretend we are talking with our parents and they ask several questions at once. "Do you want to have a friend over for the weekend? How about liver and lima beans for dinner? Would you like me to dye half your hair purple? If you were asked these questions quickly and then simply answered yes, it may get confusing, did you mean yes for all or yes to one or two? A complete sentence will clarify.
- Offer students the sentence segments page and explain they are to make a complete sentence out of the segment given. As long as

the segment is used and the sentence is complete, the actual sentence topic is not of importance.

Assessment: Grading should be based on using the given segment to create a complete sentence including punctuation.

Sample segments:

little brown dog

large box

purple ball

yellow shirt

yes, I can

raining outside

spelling test

SL 2.6 Lesson Two

Title: Build A Sentence

Topic: Creating complete sentences

Objective of lesson: Students will create unique, complete sentences from site words

Common Core State Standard used: W.2.6: Produce complete sentences when appropriate to task and situation in order to provide requested detail or clarification.

Materials needed:

Sight words on cards (A list will also work)

Time for lesson: 30-45 minutes

Lesson: (small groups)

- Separate students into small groups
- Allow students to choose two sight words or assign at least two words to each student (choose three for a challenge)
- Tell students they must use the two sight words and come up with a single complete sentence to share with the group.
- Take turns sharing a sentence using the provided words.

Assessment: Grading should be based on speaking a complete sentence using the given site words.

L 2.1 Lesson One

Title: Moose or Meece

Topic: Using irregular plurals

Objective of lesson: Students will properly place irregular plurals

Common Core State Standard used: L.2.1: Demonstrate command of the conventions of standard English grammar and usage when writing or speaking.

- CCSS.ELA-Literacy.L.2.1a Use collective nouns (e.g., *group*).
- CCSS.ELA-Literacy.L.2.1b Form and use frequently occurring irregular plural nouns (e.g.,*feet, children, teeth, mice, fish*).
- CCSS.ELA-Literacy.L.2.1c Use reflexive pronouns (e.g., *myself, ourselves*).
- CCSS.ELA-Literacy.L.2.1d Form and use the past tense of frequently occurring irregular verbs (e.g., *sat, hid, told*).
- CCSS.ELA-Literacy.L.2.1e Use adjectives and adverbs, and choose between them depending on what is to be modified.
- CCSS.ELA-Literacy.L.2.1f Produce, expand, and rearrange complete simple and compound sentences (e.g., *The boy watched the movie; The little boy watched the movie; The action movie was watched by the little boy*).

Materials needed:

Index cards (Sample terms to place on each provided)

Chalk or white board with singular version of words written

Tape or magnets (depending on board)

Time for lesson: 20-30 minutes

Lesson:

- Draw students attention to the singular nouns on the board
- Explain that some nouns are made plural by adding -s or -es, but a few are irregular, meaning they do not follow the rules of English. The terms on the board are irregular.
- Offer an example: If I have one mouse it is called a mouse, but if I have two are they called mouses? No. What are they called? Mice, good.
- Call one child at a time to the board and allow them to fill in an answer. They can choose from the cards that are taped to the board.

Assessment: Grading should be based on participation and correct answers.

Sample nouns:

Moose	Meece	Deer	Deers
Mouses	Mice	Fish	Feesh
Foots	Feet	Tooths	Teeth
Children	Childs	Sheeps	Sheep
Men	Mens	Womans	Women
Wifes	Wives	Lifes	Lives

L 2.1 Lesson Two

Title: Explore Your Past

Topic: Using irregular verbs

Objective of lesson: Students will form and use irregular verbs correctly

Common Core State Standard used: L.2.1: Demonstrate command of the conventions of standard English grammar and usage when writing or speaking.

- CCSS.ELA-Literacy.L.2.1a Use collective nouns (e.g., *group*).
- CCSS.ELA-Literacy.L.2.1b Form and use frequently occurring irregular plural nouns (e.g.,*feet, children, teeth, mice, fish*).
- CCSS.ELA-Literacy.L.2.1c Use reflexive pronouns (e.g., *myself, ourselves*).
- CCSS.ELA-Literacy.L.2.1d Form and use the past tense of frequently occurring irregular verbs (e.g., *sat, hid, told*).
- CCSS.ELA-Literacy.L.2.1e Use adjectives and adverbs, and choose between them depending on what is to be modified.
- CCSS.ELA-Literacy.L.2.1f Produce, expand, and rearrange complete simple and compound sentences (e.g., *The boy watched the movie; The little boy watched the movie; The action movie was watched by the little boy*).

Materials needed:

Timer

Paper

Worksheet (included)

Time for lesson: 20-30 minutes

Lesson:

- This should be used after you have introduced irregular verbs with the students.
- Offer students the worksheet and tell them that every word listed is an irregular verb, which means we cannot just add -ed to make it past tense. Complete one example for the group.
- Next set the timer for three minutes and have students write as many of the past tense irregular verbs as possible. Tell them not to worry if they do not get completely finished, but to keep working the whole time.
- After the timer goes off, have students check their pages.
- Now allow time to use at least ten of the words in complete sentences.

Assessment: Grading should be based on using irregular verbs correctly in sentences.

Sample Worksheet:

Become =

Begin =

Beat=

Break =

Build =

Buy =

Catch =

Cut =

Dig =

Dive =

Find =

Get =

Hang =

Hide =

Hold =

Lay =

Lie =

Leave =

Make =

Mistake =

Pay =

Grow =

Wear =

Say =

Sell =

Shoot =

Sit =

Slide =

Sing =

Speed =

Spin =

Stink =

Take =

Tell =

Win =

Wind =

L 2.2 Lesson One

Title: Capital Idea

Topic: Proper noun capitalization

Objective of lesson: Students will demonstrate correct capitalization of proper nouns when found in a sentence.

- Common Core State Standard used: L.2.2: Demonstrate command of the conventions of standard English capitalization, punctuation, and spelling when writing.
    - CCSS.ELA-Literacy.L.2.2a Capitalize holidays, product names, and geographic names.
    - CCSS.ELA-Literacy.L.2.2b Use commas in greetings and closings of letters.
    - CCSS.ELA-Literacy.L.2.2c Use an apostrophe to form contractions and frequently occurring possessives.
    - CCSS.ELA-Literacy.L.2.2d Generalize learned spelling patterns when writing words (e.g.,*cage → badge; boy → boil*).
    - CCSS.ELA-Literacy.L.2.2e Consult reference materials, including beginning dictionaries, as needed to check and correct spellings.

Materials needed:

White board

Projector

Document with sentences to rewrite (Sample included)

Time for lesson: 15-20 minutes (depending on number of students)

Lesson:

- Remind students of what types of nouns are considered proper (a name, a place, a holiday).
- Tell students that you are going to show them some sentences that have proper nouns that are not capitalized.
- One at a time, have students correct a proper noun in a sentence. Allow students to correct any proper nouns they see, even if it is not in order.

Assessment: Grading should be based on correctly identifying and correcting proper nouns.

Sample Sentences:

1) On christmas eve we all meet at my grandmother's house to open gifts.

2) The dog's name was stanley, but we all called him stan for short.

3) The substitute teacher said to call her ms. Calvert.

4) Every year on thanksgiving we serve food at the soup kitchen.

5) Dover, denver, and cleveland are all cities in the united states.

6) The first time I ever rode on an airplane it was called the concorde.

7) Will you be riding the bus to washington with us?

8) Mrs. jenkins loves to talk about her favorite holidays, easter, halloween, and valentine's day.

9) When I go to the mall I like to shop at k-mart, khols, and petland.

10) I have visited arkansas, West virginia, and colorado.

11) When we went on vacation we went to disney world and epcot.

12) Do you want to be called Michael or mike?

L 2.2 Lesson Two

Title: Shorten It

Topic: Creating contractions

Objective of lesson: Students will create contractions

Common Core State Standard used: L.2.2: Demonstrate command of the conventions of standard English capitalization, punctuation, and spelling when writing.

- CCSS.ELA-Literacy.L.2.2a Capitalize holidays, product names, and geographic names.
- CCSS.ELA-Literacy.L.2.2b Use commas in greetings and closings of letters.
- CCSS.ELA-Literacy.L.2.2c Use an apostrophe to form contractions and frequently occurring possessives.
- CCSS.ELA-Literacy.L.2.2d Generalize learned spelling patterns when writing words (e.g.,*cage → badge; boy → boil*).
- CCSS.ELA-Literacy.L.2.2e Consult reference materials, including beginning dictionaries, as needed to check and correct spellings.

Materials needed:

List of word cards (Included) *Copies can be made as needed

Timer

Time for lesson: 30-45 minutes

Lesson:

- Remind students that when writing, there are times when we can combine two words to make one shorter word, these are called contractions. To hold the two words together, we must replace the missing letters with an apostrophe. Apostrophes can stand for one letter or several.
- Hand out cards to students in a random manner. Tell them not to look at the cards until you turn on the timer. Explain that when you turn on the timer they will have 60 seconds to find their partners and line up in order. For example can + not = can't All three partners need to be found.
- Have students find a partner that has a word with which they can make a contraction and then a third person who has the contraction completed.
- Have students do this activity several times. Write several contractions on the board.
- Students can choose 5 contractions and write their own sentences.

Assessment: Grading should be based on correctly finding all three people and linking in the correct order.

Can	Not	Can't
Do	Not	Don't
Will	Not	Won't
Should	Not	Shouldn't
Would	Not	Wouldn't
Could	Have	Should've
Would	Have	Would've
Did	Not	Didn't

L 2.3 Lesson One

Title: Talk Right

Topic: Formal communications

Objective of lesson: Students will listen to the difference in speaking formally versus informally

Common Core State Standard used: L.2.3: Use knowledge of language and its conventions when writing, speaking, reading, or listening.

- CCSS.ELA-Literacy.L.2.3a Compare formal and informal uses of English

Materials needed:

Time for lesson: 30-45 minutes

Lesson:

- Explain to students that there are times when you must speak in a different manner, more formally. People speak in a formal manner when discussing things with another professional or someone older or even when meeting someone for the first time.
- Ask students to think about telling a story to their friends. Now ask them to think about telling a story to the principal. Speaking to the principal should be formal, but with friends we can be informal.

- Offer an example: Informal: Hey guys do you want to come to my house for a party this weekend? Formal: We would like to invite you to a party at my home this weekend. Would you like to attend?
- Try several other examples to allow children to guess if it is formal or informal. Allow them to try speaking in both manners with a partner.
- Have students create their own writing that expresses both formal and informal.

Assessment: Grading should be based on participation and partner work if time permits.

L 2.3 Lesson Two

Title: Read Aloud

Topic: Reading with purpose

Objective of lesson: Students will read aloud within small groups

Common Core State Standard used: L.2.3: Use knowledge of language and its conventions when writing, speaking, reading, or listening.

- CCSS.ELA-Literacy.L.2.3a Compare formal and informal uses of English

Materials needed:

Sets of books for small groups

Time for lesson: 10-15 minutes

Lesson:

- Gather students in small groups with identical books for each group member.
- Have students take turns reading aloud in an appropriate manner. To make sure students are paying attention tell each student they must read one full line, but then they can pick the next reader anytime they wish, even in the middle of a sentence.

Assessment: Grading should be based on reading in a correct manner.

L 2.4 Lesson One

Title: This Or That

Topic: Clarifying meaning of multiple-meaning words

Objective of lesson: Students will draw illustrations to clarify the meaning of multiple meaning words.

Common Core State Standard used: L.2.4: Determine or clarify the meaning of unknown and multiple-meaning words and phrases based on grade 2 reading and content, choosing flexibly from an array of strategies.

- CCSS.ELA-Literacy.L.2.4a Use sentence-level context as a clue to the meaning of a word or phrase.
- CCSS.ELA-Literacy.L.2.4b Determine the meaning of the new word formed when a known prefix is added to a known word (e.g., *happy/unhappy, tell/retell*).
- CCSS.ELA-Literacy.L.2.4c Use a known root word as a clue to the meaning of an unknown word with the same root (e.g., *addition, additional*).
- CCSS.ELA-Literacy.L.2.4d Use knowledge of the meaning of individual words to predict the meaning of compound words (e.g., *birdhouse, lighthouse, housefly; bookshelf, notebook, bookmark*).
- CCSS.ELA-Literacy.L.2.4e Use glossaries and beginning dictionaries, both print and digital, to determine or clarify the meaning of words and phrases.

Materials needed:

Art supplies

List of dual meaning words

Time for lesson: 45-60 minutes

Lesson:

- Begin by asking students what a bat is. Some will say what you use in baseball to hit the ball while others may say an animal that flies at night.
- Tell students that there are many words that have two or more meanings.
- Share the list of words with students and then give them a sheet of long drawing paper
- Have students fold the paper in half lengthwise (hotdog) and then into thirds width wise(hamburger), creating six boxes when unfolded. Each box will hold a picture that defines one meaning of the given word, the second meaning can be drawn under the first picture. The child should then write the meanings of the words out under the corresponding picture (sample shown). Students can draw on the front and back.

Assessment: Grading should be based on drawings that correctly identify meaning.

Word List (Not all words will be used):

Cap	Board
Dance	Color
Pet	Fish
Bowl	Roll

Sample Paper:

Cap as in hat

Bowl as in dish

This flower is the color purple

Cap as in lid

Bowl as in the game

I color with crayons

L 2.4 Lesson Two

Title: If This, Than That

Topic: Using known words to decipher compound words

Objective of lesson: Students will draw illustrations to show meaning of compound words

Common Core State Standard used: L.2.4: Determine or clarify the meaning of unknown and multiple-meaning words and phrases based on grade 2 reading and content, choosing flexibly from an array of strategies.

- CCSS.ELA-Literacy.L.2.4a Use sentence-level context as a clue to the meaning of a word or phrase.
- CCSS.ELA-Literacy.L.2.4b Determine the meaning of the new word formed when a known prefix is added to a known word (e.g., *happy/unhappy, tell/retell*).
- CCSS.ELA-Literacy.L.2.4c Use a known root word as a clue to the meaning of an unknown word with the same root (e.g., *addition, additional*).
- CCSS.ELA-Literacy.L.2.4d Use knowledge of the meaning of individual words to predict the meaning of compound words (e.g., *birdhouse, lighthouse, housefly; bookshelf, notebook, bookmark*).
- CCSS.ELA-Literacy.L.2.4e Use glossaries and beginning dictionaries, both print and digital, to determine or clarify the meaning of words and phrases.

Materials needed:

Art supplies

Supplied worksheet

Time for lesson: 20-30 minutes

Lesson:

- Have students read two common words on the board, something like dog and house. Ask what happens if you combine these words. You get a compound word, doghouse, with a new meaning.
- Explain that you are going to give them some words with pictures that are to be combined into a compound word. Not all the compound words will be real things, but you want to test their combining ability.
- Show the example on the worksheet.

Assessment: Grading should be based on drawings show the two words were combined, not whether the final drawing is accurate.

Worksheet:

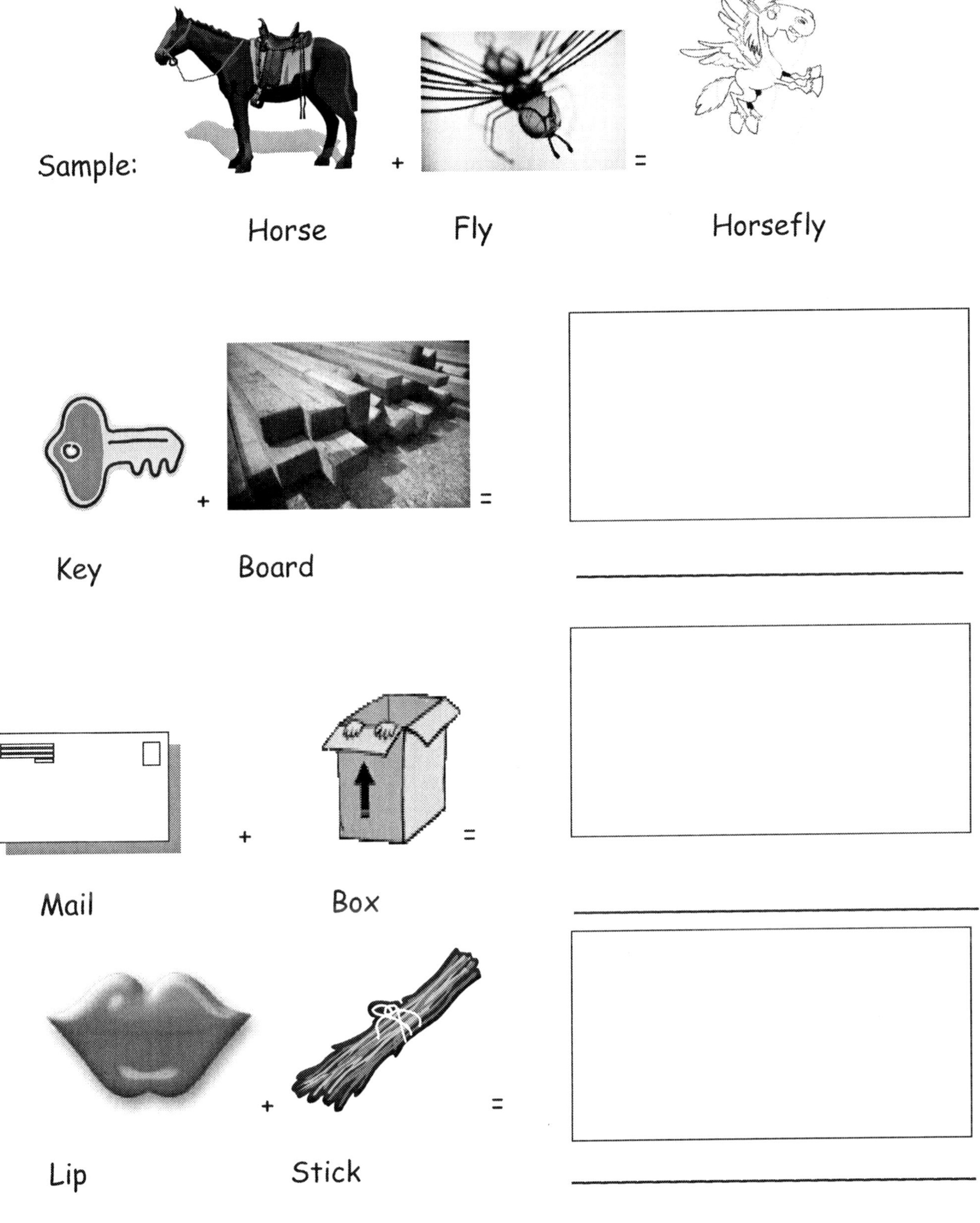

L 2.5 Lesson One

Title: Describe It For Me

Topic: Descriptive terminology

Objective of lesson: Students will demonstrate knowledge of descriptive terms.

Common Core Standard used: L 2.5: Demonstrate understanding of figurative language, word relationships and nuances in word meanings.

- CCSS.ELA-Literacy.L.2.5a Identify real-life connections between words and their use (e.g.,*describe foods that are spicy or juicy*).
- CCSS.ELA-Literacy.L.2.5b Distinguish shades of meaning among closely related verbs (e.g.,*toss, throw, hurl*) and closely related adjectives (e.g., *thin, slender, skinny, scrawny*).

Materials needed:

Art supplies including magazines or other sources for pictures to be cut out.

List of terms.

Time for lesson: 45-60 minutes

Lesson:

- Begin this lesson with a question: Who can point to something in this room that is hard? Allow students to point.
- Explain to students that descriptive words help make what we read and write clearer, but we have to know what those descriptive terms mean.
- Ask another example. Who can name a food that is spicy? Take answers.
- Explain to students that you are going to give them some descriptive terms and some magazines. They are to find a picture that represents each descriptive term and then write that term under the picture. The pictures can be in any order and can be big or small as long as they are all on the page (Collage style if you wish).

Assessment: Grading should be based on finding a picture to accurately represent the given descriptive term.

Sample Descriptive Terms:

Hot	Slimy
Cold	Tiny
Soft	Bright
Shiny	Angry
Tasty	Hard

L 2.5 Lesson Two

Title: Big, Huge, Monster

Topic: Descriptive, related verbs

Objective of lesson: Students will demonstrate knowledge of related verbs.

Common Core Standard used: L 2.5: Demonstrate understanding of figurative language, word relationships and nuances in word meanings.

- CCSS.ELA-Literacy.L.2.5a Identify real-life connections between words and their use (e.g.,*describe foods that are spicy or juicy*).
- CCSS.ELA-Literacy.L.2.5b Distinguish shades of meaning among closely related verbs (e.g.,*toss, throw, hurl*) and closely related adjectives (e.g., *thin, slender, skinny, scrawny*).

Materials needed:

Toy or other common classroom items need to be readily available

Time for lesson: 30-45 minutes

Lesson:

- Tell children that they are going to visually demonstrate related verbs. Offer the example of big, huge, monstrous and use blocks to show the size differences.

- Offer children sets of words and allow them to find objects around the room to represent the words.

Assessment: Grading should be based on being able to distinguish the related verb.

Related Word Samples:

Tiny, small, miniscule

Big, large, enormous

Small, large, medium

Thin, wide, medium

Short, medium, long

Tall, short, average

Toss, throw, hurl

Walk, skip, slide

Low, high, eye-level

Fold, bend, break

Circle, sphere, oval

L 2.6 Lesson One

Title: Adding Adjectives

Topic: Adjective use

Objective of lesson: Students will add appropriate adjectives to sentences.

Common Core Standard used: L 2.6: Use words and phrases acquired through conversations, reading and being read to, and responding to texts, including using adjectives and adverbs to describe (e.g., *When other kids are happy that makes me happy*).

Materials needed:

Sentence strips

Index cards

Markers

Timer

Tape or sticky putty

Time for lesson: 30-45 minutes

Lesson:

- Write sentences on sentence strips that have a blank for an adjective. Make sure several different adjectives would work in the spot.

- Give each student a marker and enough index cards to write one adjective for each sentence.
- Set the timer for five minutes (less if only a few sentences are used) and tell students they must provide one descriptive word (adjective) per sentence and tape it on the wall. Also tell students that if the adjective has been used, they need think of a different one.
- Have students share which word they added to the sentences by reading the sentence aloud.

Assessment: Grading should be based on appropriate adjective and participation.

L 2.6 Lesson Two

Title: Mad Libs Adjective Style

Topic: Adjective use

Objective of lesson: Students will add appropriate adjectives to create a funny story.

Common Core Standard used: L 2.6: Use words and phrases acquired through conversations, reading and being read to, and responding to texts, including using adjectives and adverbs to describe (e.g., *When other kids are happy that makes me happy*).

Materials needed:

Mad Lib (Sample included)

Writing utensil

Time for lesson: 20-30 minutes

Lesson: (Singles, small, or large group)

- Have students fill in adjectives only to create a fun story.
- Have students share their stories with a small group or the whole class depending on time allowed.

Assessment: Grading should be based on providing appropriate adjectives.

Sample Mad Lib:

There once was a ________ elephant that was afraid of __________ mice. This elephant was so afraid that he hid in his ___________ house most of the day and night. One day as he was cleaning his ______________ room, he heard a _____________ sound. The sound was coming from a corner. He glanced over to see a ________ mouse climbing up his _____________ table. The elephant reacted __________. He screamed like a little girl and took off running through the enclosure. As he flew passed all the _________ trees, he glanced up at the ___________leaves. Suddenly the elephant slowed down and really looked around. He felt the earth under his _________________ feet and the _____________ sun on his _______________ ears. He stopped cold. It then occurred to the elephant that there was much more to be afraid of than a ___________ mouse. ______________ elephant, he doesn't know much of anything.

Mathematics

OA.A 2.1 Lesson One

Title: Work It Out

Topic: Addition word problems

Objective of lesson: Students will complete addition word problems with the use of drawings.

Common Core Standard used: OA.A 2.1: Use addition and subtraction within 100 to solve one- and two-step word problems involving situations of adding to, taking from, putting together, taking apart, and comparing, with unknowns in all positions, e.g., by using drawings and equations with a symbol for the unknown number to represent the problem.

Materials needed:

Addition word problems

Time for lesson: 30-45 minutes

Lesson:

- Explain to students that when doing word problems it often helps to draw pictures to help solve the problem.
- Offer students the included word problems and have them draw pictures to represent each problem.
- Students will share their pictures with the class.
- Make sure to display pictures to help kids with word problems in the future.

Assessment: Grading should be based on correct answers and accompanying drawings.

Sample Word Problems:

1) Angie had 14 apples from a tree in her back yard. Sarah had 19 oranges from her back yard. Jimmy had 3 bunches of bananas with 22 bananas total. How many total pieces of fruit did the trio have?

2) A farm had several animals. In fact it had 6 chickens, 4 horses, 3 dogs, 2 cows, and a pet cat. If you count up all the legs on all the animals, how many legs would there be on the farm?

3) An octopus has eight tentacles. A starfish has five arms. If I have five octopi, how many tentacles would I see?

4) A star has five points. A triangle has three points. If I have 5 stars and 3 triangles, how many points will I have?

5) My mother has to make cupcakes for the party. She wants everyone to have only one cupcake. She makes cupcakes by the dozen. There are 12 cupcakes in each dozen. How many dozen cupcakes will need to be made to feed 36 people?

6) My teacher left the rulers out one day. Each ruler is 1 foot long. If I lay 50 rulers end to end, how many feet will they stretch?

7) Finn loves dog treats, so I bought her a big box. There are 50 bones that taste like chicken, 30 that taste like beef, and 20 that taste like vegetables. How many bones are in Finn's treat box?

OA.A 2.1 Lesson Two

Title: Journal It

Topic: Creating word problems

Objective of lesson: Students will create addition and subtraction word problems.

Common Core Standard used: OA.A 2.1: Use addition and subtraction within 100 to solve one- and two-step word problems involving situations of adding to, taking from, putting together, taking apart, and comparing, with unknowns in all positions, e.g., by using drawings and equations with a symbol for the unknown number to represent the problem.

Materials needed:

Journals

Time for lesson: 5-8 minutes (per day)

Lesson:

- Explain to students that they are going to start keeping math journals. A math journal is only for math problems. Each day you will challenge them to create addition, subtraction, or word problems.
- After students have had time to create at least two problems each day, choose two or three students to write their problems on the board and share how to arrive at the answer.

- Students can add problems to their math journal several times throughout the school year.

Assessment: Grading should be based on journal entries and solving problems.

Sample Problems:

Day 1: Write two problems that have the solution of 25

Day 2: Write two addition word problems

Day 3: Write two subtraction problems

Day 4: Write one subtraction word problem and one addition word problem

Day 5: Write two problems that have at least three numbers

Day 6: Write two math problems that have both addition and subtraction in them (ie 3+2-1=4)

Day 7:Write two math problems that have a solution that ends in 5

OA.B 2.2 Lesson One

Title: Minute Math

Topic: Adding and subtracting within 20

Objective of lesson: Students will add and subtract within 20 using mental strategies.

Common Core Standard used: OA.B 2.2: Fluently add and subtract within 20 using mental strategies. By end of Grade 2, know from memory all sums of two one-digit numbers.

Materials needed:

Minute Math work sheets

Timer

Time for lesson: 1 minute per day

Lesson:

- Explain to students that practice makes perfect, especially when it comes to math.
- Tell students to place the Minute Math on their desk face down until you say go.
- Set the timer for 60 seconds. When you say go have students complete as many problems as possible before the timer goes off.
- Grade worksheets and have students record the scores daily to watch progress.

Assessment: Grading should be based on correct answers and improvement over time.

Sample Minute Math: (Shuffle problem order or problems so students are doing math not memorizing order)

4+ 5 =	7+ 10 =	19 - 2=	18+ 2 =
14 - 4 =	9 + 3 =	11+ 7 =	20 - 6=
8+ 4 =	2-2=	17 - 3=	19 - 6=
6+ 9=	12 - 3=	18 - 7=	20 -20=
2+7=	9+11=	5 + 6=	13 + 4=
9 + 7 =	10 - 0=	0 + 7=	6 + 13 =
3 + 2 =	4 - 3 =	7 - 5=	20 - 10=
1 -1 =	18 + 2=	18 - 2=	5 + 9 =

OA.B 2.2 Lesson Two

Title: Mental Math

Topic: Adding and subtracting within 20

Objective of lesson: Students will add and subtract within 20 using mental strategies.

Common Core Standard used: OA.B 2.2: Fluently add and subtract within 20 using mental strategies. By end of Grade 2, know from memory all sums of two one-digit numbers.

Materials needed:

List of problems to choose from

Time for lesson: 5-10 minute per day

Lesson:

- Have students stand by their desk or in a line in the classroom
- Call out a problem and a name and have the student answer, this is all about speed and accuracy

Assessment: Grading should be based on correct answers.

OA.C 2.3 Lesson One

Title: Odds Or Evens

Topic: Determining odd and even numbers

Objective of lesson: Students will identify whether numbers are odd or even through pairing

Common Core Standard used: OA.C 2.3: Determine whether a group of objects (up to 20) has an odd or even number of members, e.g., by pairing objects or counting them by 2s; write an equation to express an even number as a sum of two equal addends.

Materials needed:

Manipulatives (blocks, paper clips, shapes, straws, etc.)

Odds/Evens triangle (Template included)

Time for lesson: 15-20 minutes

Lesson:

- Provide each child with at least twenty manipulative, children can have different types.
- Ask children how many of something is in a pair. Two.
- Call out a number between 1-20 and have children count out that number of object.
- Have children pair objects off. If everything has a pair then the student should turn the even card facing forward, if something is left without a pair, the odd card should face forward.

Assessment: Grading should be based on correct answers and correct pairing.

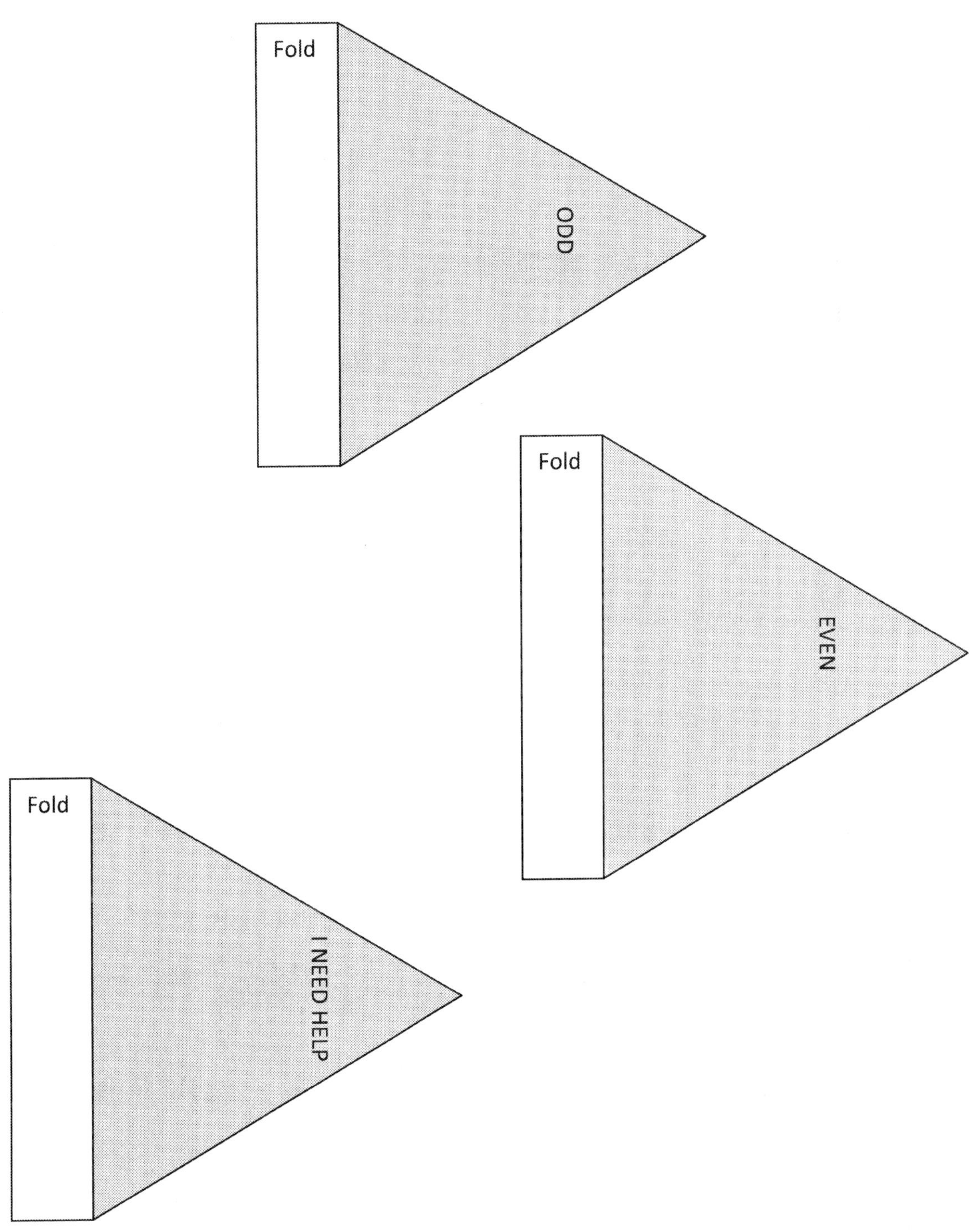

OA.C 2.3 Lesson Two

Title: Toss It

Topic: Determining odd and even numbers

Objective of lesson: Students will identify whether numbers are odd or even

Common Core Standard used: OA.C 2.3: Determine whether a group of objects (up to 20) has an odd or even number of members, e.g., by pairing objects or counting them by 2s; write an equation to express an even number as a sum of two equal addends.

Materials needed:

Two baskets or buckets (Labeled odd and even)

Ping pong balls (Labeled 1-20)

Masking tape (Three lines, varying distances from the baskets)

Time for lesson: 15-20 minutes

Lesson:

- Great warm activity.
- Separate the class into two or three teams. Explain to students that they will take turns on their teams to choose a ball (without looking).
- After the child sees the number they must announce whether it is odd or even, if correct give the team a point.

- Next have that child try to toss the ball into the correct basket. They may choose whether to stand on the 1, 2, or 3 point line to try. A basket gets that number of points, a miss gets nothing.
- The team with the most points wins. Place numbers back in with ping pong balls to give more chances to try.

Assessment: Grading should be based choosing the correct basket to aim for with the given number.

OA.D 2.4 Lesson One

Title: Add It Up

Topic: Using rectangular arrays to create

Objective of lesson: Students will create math problems based on a given rectangular array.

Common Core Standard used: OA.D 2.4: Use addition to find the total number of objects arranged in rectangular arrays with up to 5 rows and up to 5 columns; write an equation to express the total as a sum of equal addends.

Materials needed:

Time for lesson: 15 minutes

Lesson:

- Explain to students that math problems can be created by rectangular arrays. A rectangular array is simply a design in the shape of a rectangle. The columns and rows can be added to get a sum.
- Offer this example on the board 5 + 5 + 5 = (count the boxes)

•	•	•	•	•
•	•	•	•	•
•	•	•	•	•

- Have students solve the example. Explain that they will be both writing the problem and solving it for given rectangular arrays.

Assessment: Grading should be based offering a valid math problem and correct solution.

Sample Arrays:

1	1
1	1
1	1
1	1

@	@	@	@
@	@	@	@
@	@	@	@

O	O	O
O	O	O
O	O	O

?	?	?	?	?
?	?	?	?	?

OA.D 2.4 Lesson Two

Title: Draw It Out

Topic: Using math problems to create rectangular arrays

Objective of lesson: Students will create rectangular arrays based on math problems.

Common Core Standard used: OA.D 2.4: Use addition to find the total number of objects arranged in rectangular arrays with up to 5 rows and up to 5 columns; write an equation to express the total as a sum of equal addends.

Materials needed:

Time for lesson: 20-30 minutes

Lesson:

- Explain to students that a rectangular array is a visual way of showing a math problem. Give the following example: 5 + 5 + 5 can be shown as

•	•	•
•	•	•
•	•	•
•	•	•
•	•	•

or as

•	•	•	•	•
•	•	•	•	•
•	•	•	•	•

Both are representations that would work.

- Explain that students will be given several math problems and they are to draw rectangular arrays (always rectangular) to represent those problems and then solve.
- Have students work in small groups and they are to give each other new problems to create arrays. They can put these problems in their math journal.

Assessment: Grading should be based offering a valid rectangular array and correct solution to the problem.

Sample Math Problems:

5 + 5 + 5 + 5 =

3 + 3 =

2 + 2 + 2 + 2 =

1 + 1 + 1 =

4 + 4 =

3 + 3 + 3 + 3 =

2 + 2 + 2 =

NBT.A 2.1 Lesson One

Title: Bundle Up

Topic: Grouping tens to make hundreds

Objective of lesson: Students will bundle correct groups of ten tens bundles to create hundreds (ie 5 ten tens bundles to make 500)

- Common Core Standard used: NBT.A 2.1: Understand that the three digits of a three-digit number represent amounts of hundreds, tens, and ones; e.g., 706 equals 7 hundreds, 0 tens, and 6 ones. Understand the following as special cases:
    - CCSS.Math.Content.2.NBT.A.1a 100 can be thought of as a bundle of ten tens — called a "hundred."
    - CCSS.Math.Content.2.NBT.A.1b The numbers 100, 200, 300, 400, 500, 600, 700, 800, 900 refer to one, two, three, four, five, six, seven, eight, or nine hundreds (and 0 tens and 0 ones).

Materials needed:

Rubber bands

Straws

Time for lesson: 10-15 minutes (per group)

Lesson: (small groups)

- Explain to students that 100 ones make one hundred, but 10 bunches of ten ones also make one hundred. Count the straws out in both ways to show your point.
- Now tell students that they are going to bundle straws in groups of ten. Allow students to bundle all straws in groups of ten.
- Ask students how many bundles of ten are in one hundred: 10: Good now if we put a rubber band around 10 tens bundles we will have 100. How many times would we need to make these bundles to get 300?
- Continue in this manner

Assessment: Grading should be based the ability to create groups of tens and hundreds in appropriate amounts.

NBT.A 2.1 Lesson Two

Title: Blocked Up

Topic: Understanding groups of tens can make hundreds

Objective of lesson: Students will create a visual to understand tens groups can be used to make hundreds.

- Common Core Standard used: NBT.A 2.1: Understand that the three digits of a three-digit number represent amounts of hundreds, tens, and ones; e.g., 706 equals 7 hundreds, 0 tens, and 6 ones. Understand the following as special cases:
    - CCSS.Math.Content.2.NBT.A.1a 100 can be thought of as a bundle of ten tens — called a "hundred."
    - CCSS.Math.Content.2.NBT.A.1b The numbers 100, 200, 300, 400, 500, 600, 700, 800, 900 refer to one, two, three, four, five, six, seven, eight, or nine hundreds (and 0 tens and 0 ones).

Materials needed:

Math blocks in ones, tens, hundreds

Time for lesson: 20-45 minutes

Lesson:

- Give students several base ten blocks in all sets (ones, tens, and hundreds) Have students hold up a ones block, then a tens block, and then a hundreds block. Ask how many ones blocks would fit on the tens blocks.

- Have students lay the ones blocks on the tens block to check their answer.
- Now ask how many tens blocks it would take to cover the hundreds block. Allow time for students to check the answer by covering the hundreds block.
- Have students repeat the process with 200, 300, etc. to further understanding.
- Practice over several days.

Assessment: Grading should be based on participation and understanding.

NBT.B 2.2 Lesson One

Title: Count Me In

Topic: Skip counting

Objective of lesson: Students will skip count by 5s, 10s, and 100s

Common Core Standard used: NBT.B 2.2: Count within 1000; skip-count by 5s, 10s, and 100s.

Materials needed:

Outdoor chalk

Time for lesson: 15-30 minutes

Lesson:

- Explain to students they are going to create their own numbers chart.
- Allow students to go outdoors and create number charts or lines of numbers in which they count by 5s, 10s, or 100s

Assessment: Grading should be based on participation and correct counting.

* A water hose will easily erase all the writing*

NBT.B 2.2 Lesson Two

Title: Change It Up

Topic: Skip counting

Objective of lesson: Students will skip count by 5s and 10s

Common Core Standard used: NBT.B 2.2: Count within 1000; skip-count by 5s, 10s, and 100s.

Materials needed:

Change

Change wrappers

Time for lesson: 20-30 minutes - counting time

Lesson:

- Begin by sending a note home to parents that the students are practicing skip counting while working toward an extra special treat like cake and ice cream or extended recess.
- Have students bring in only dimes and nickels to collect and help fund the extra treat.
- Once a set container is full, have students sort out the money and count it out by fives or tens to reach the amount needed to fill the wrapper (200 for nickels, 500 for dimes)

- Once money is counted use it toward the promised gift or if no food or prizes are allowed, donate money and allow for extra playtime.

Assessment: Grading should be based on counting correctly.

NBT.B 2.3 Lesson One

Title: Expandable Numbers

Topic: Expanding numbers

Objective of lesson: Students will write out expanded forms of given numbers.

Common Core Standard used: NBT.B 2.3: Read and write numbers to 1000 using base-ten numerals, number names, and expanded form.

Materials needed:

Strips of paper

Markers

Time for lesson: 30-45 minutes

Lesson:

- Explain to students that numbers can be expanded, sort of like what we would add together to get a total, but by ones, tens, hundreds, and thousands place holders.
- Give the following example: 2,156 can be expanded to 2000, 100, 50, and 6. This is the expanded form.
- Now have students select several strips of paper (one for each expanded number you want written).
- Have students write a given number space out on the paper strip, and then fill in the expanded version. (Example provided)

- Students can work in pairs or small groups.
- Have students fold the paper (as shown) so that the simple version is viewable, then expand to see expanded version. Continue for desired numbers.

Assessment: Grading should be based on accurately expanding numbers.

1	000	3	00	6	0	9

Fold on the lines (1,369)

NBT.B 2.3 Lesson Two

Title: Read Aloud Math

Topic: Reading number names

Objective of lesson: Students will read aloud numbers that are printed on the board

Common Core Standard used: NBT.B 2.3: Read and write numbers to 1000 using base-ten numerals, number names, and expanded form.

Materials needed:

Chalk or white board

Time for lesson: 5-10 minutes

Lesson:

- Use this as a warm up activity.
- Write several numbers on the board.
- At random choose a student to say the number out loud in the correct manner. Example: 1,234 would be read as One thousand two hundred thirty four.

Assessment: Grading should be based on accurately reading numbers.

NBT.B 2.4 Lesson One

Title: Feed The Gator

Topic: Determining greater than, less than, or equal to with three digit numbers

Objective of lesson: Students will compare three digit numbers, determining which is greater than the other

Common Core Standard used: NBT.B 2.4: Compare two three-digit numbers based on meanings of the hundreds, tens, and ones digits, using >, =, and < symbols to record the results of comparisons.

Materials needed:

Toy alligator

Paper circles with numbers on them

Time for lesson: 5-10 minutes

Lesson: (Small groups)

- Explain to students that they are going to practice math while feeding alligators. Remind students that alligators only want the biggest meals.
- Have students randomly choose two number circles.
- Next have students place the alligator so that his mouth points to the larger of the two numbers.

Assessment: Grading should be based on accurately pointing the alligator mouth toward the larger number.

NBT.B 2.4 Lesson Two

Title: Close Calls

Topic: Determining greater than, less than, or equal to with three digit numbers

Objective of lesson: Students will compare three digit numbers, determining which is greater than the other with closely related numbers.

Common Core Standard used: NBT.B 2.4: Compare two three-digit numbers based on meanings of the hundreds, tens, and ones digits, using >, =, and < symbols to record the results of comparisons.

Materials needed:

Worksheet (Included)

Time for lesson: 10-15 minutes

Lesson:

- Explain to students that sometimes we must look very closely at numbers to know which is bigger and which is smaller.
- Have students complete the worksheet by pointing the arrow toward the smaller number.
- Have students work with partners and create their own problems. Encourage students to add problems to their math journal.

Assessment: Grading should be based on accurately demonstrating less than, equal to, or greater than.

Sample Worksheet:

318 _____ 322	156 ____ 175
56 ____ 103	562 ____ 462
107 ____ 207	333 ____ 332
411 ____ 512	100 ____ 200
321 ____ 321	57 ____ 157
123 ____ 321	129 ____ 301
103 ____103	77 ____ 107
145 ____154	246 ____240

NBT.B 2.5 Lesson One

Title: Choose Your Strategy

Topic: Addition and subtraction

Objective of lesson: Students will add and subtract numbers within 100

Common Core Standard used: NBT.B 2.5: Fluently add and subtract within 100 using strategies based on place value, properties of operations, and/or the relationship between addition and subtraction.

Materials needed:

Math problems (addition and subtraction)

Access to supplies needed for math strategies

Time for lesson: 10-20 minutes

Lesson:

- Explain to students that there are many ways to solve addition and subtraction problems. We can count on our fingers, use TouchPoint math, use a number line, draw objects, or use actual objects.
- Tell students you are going to give them a worksheet or problems to solve and you want them to use the different strategies they know to solve.
- Allow children access to supplies as needed.

Assessment: Grading should be based on accurately finding solutions.

NBT.B 2.5 Lesson Two

Title: Math Basketball

Topic: Addition and subtraction

Objective of lesson: Students will add and subtract numbers within 100

Common Core Standard used: NBT.B 2.5: Fluently add and subtract within 100 using strategies based on place value, properties of operations, and/or the relationship between addition and subtraction.

Materials needed:

Math problems

Marked areas for point lines

Board with/chalk or markers

Ball

Time for lesson: 10-30 minutes

Lesson:

- Split students into two teams
- Explain to students that they will be racing to complete a math problem
- One person from each team will go to the board and a problem will be given to solve. If both people solve the problem, both teams get a point, but the person that finished first gets the opportunity to earn more points for their team.

- The person that finishes first must choose whether to shoot from the 1,2, or 3 point line. They must then try to get a small ball or wadded up paper in a trash can from that line. One shot only.
- If the ball goes in that team gets the point, if it doesn't then no points are added to either team and you go to the next set of people.

Assessment: Grading should be based on accurately finding solutions.

NBT.B 2.6 Lesson One

Title: Line 'Em Up

Topic: Addition of multiple two digit numbers

Objective of lesson: Students will add two digit numbers accurately.

Common Core Standard used: NBT.B 2.6: Add up to four two-digit numbers using strategies based on place value and properties of operations.

Materials needed:

Selection of two digit numbers

Time for lesson: 25-35 minutes

Lesson:

- Offer students a list of numbers on the board, all two digit numbers.
- Students can use small white boards, quick assessment for teacher.
- Tell students they are going to create their own math problems to solve. They can only use each number once and every problem must have at least three numbers.
- Have students create and solve problems.

Assessment: Grading should be based on accurately finding solutions as well as crating problems.

NBT.B 2.6 Lesson Two

Title: Magnet Math

Topic: Addition of multiple two digit numbers

Objective of lesson: Students will add multiple two digit numbers.

Common Core Standard used: NBT.B 2.6: Add up to four two-digit numbers using strategies based on place value and properties of operations.

Materials needed:

Selection of magnetic numbers (or number blocks)

Time for lesson: 10-15 minutes (per group)

Lesson: (small groups)

- This is a quick way to practice addition skills while keeping hands busy. Create math problems for each student in the group using number magnets.
- Have students try to solve problems and create the answer in magnets.
- Students should add addition problems in their math journal.

Assessment: Grading should be based on accurately finding solutions.

NBT.B 2.7 Lesson One

Title: Shave Off A Few Numbers

Topic: Subtraction of three digit numbers

Objective of lesson: Students will subtract three digit numbers accurately.

Common Core Standard used: NBT.B 2.7: Add and subtract within 1000, using concrete models or drawings and strategies based on place value, properties of operations, and/or the relationship between addition and subtraction; relate the strategy to a written method. Understand that in adding or subtracting three-digit numbers, one adds or subtracts hundreds and hundreds, tens and tens, ones and ones; and sometimes it is necessary to compose or decompose tens or hundreds.

Materials needed:

Shaving cream (unscented)

Large flat surfaces

Time for lesson: 10-20 minutes (per group)

Lesson: (small groups)

- This is a great way to have a sensory math lesson that students will enjoy while practicing subtraction problems.

- Call out a math problem to students using 3 digit numbers. Allow students to write the math problem in the shaving cream and solve.

Assessment: Grading should be based on accurately finding solutions and writing the numbers correctly.

NBT.B 2.7 Lesson Two

Title: Let's Go Shopping

Topic: Addition of three digit numbers

Objective of lesson: Students will add two and three digit whole numbers within 1000.

Common Core Standard used: NBT.B 2.7: Add and subtract within 1000, using concrete models or drawings and strategies based on place value, properties of operations, and/or the relationship between addition and subtraction; relate the strategy to a written method. Understand that in adding or subtracting three-digit numbers, one adds or subtracts hundreds and hundreds, tens and tens, ones and ones; and sometimes it is necessary to compose or decompose tens or hundreds.

Materials needed:

Several copies of the Toys R Us big toy book (or other like magazines)

Paper

Time for lesson: 30-45 minutes (per group)

Lesson: (small groups)

- This can be used as a follow up to a estimation lesson.
- Have students look through the catalog to find at least three toys they would like to have.
- Help students to round the price of the toy up to the next whole dollar amount.

- Have students add the selections together to see how much they need to save.
- Repeat with different numbers of toys.

Assessment: Grading should be based on accurately finding solutions.

NBT.B 2.8 Lesson One

Title: Mental Math II

Topic: Mental addition and subtraction of 10 or 100

Objective of lesson: Students will mentally add and record adding or subtracting 10's and 100's.

Common Core Standard used: NBT.B 2.8: Mentally add 10 or 100 to a given number 100-900, and mentally subtract 10 or 100 from a given number 100-900.

Materials needed:

Paper

List of problems

Time for lesson: 10-15 minutes

Lesson:

- Have students number a sheet of paper to 15.
- Explain that you are going to call out math problems that are either addition or subtraction of tens or hundreds.
- They will have 5 seconds to answer each one before you move on to the next.
- Students can follow up this activity with partners and white boards.

Assessment: Grading should be based on accurately finding solutions.

NBT.B 2.8 Lesson Two

Title: Math Twister

Topic: Mental addition and subtraction of 10 or 100

Objective of lesson: Students will mentally add or subtract 10's and 100's.

Common Core Standard used: NBT.B 2.8: Mentally add 10 or 100 to a given number 100-900, and mentally subtract 10 or 100 from a given number 100-900.

Materials needed:

Twister mat (labeled as red- ten less, blue - ten more, yellow - 100 more, green - 100 less)

Time for lesson: 10-15 minutes per group.

Lesson:

- Have ten students stand on the twister mat on their choice of colors.
- Explain that you will call out a math problem in which they must decide whether 10 or 100 has been added or subtracted. If ten has been subtracted they must find a red circle to stand on, ten added, a blue circle, etc. Students must solve quickly and find a circle as there are more students then circles.
- Give a sample problem: If I have 800 and then have 700 what happened? subtracted 100...green circle.

- Students will have to think quickly and cannot move once they have chosen a circle.
- Continue until all problems have been used or all students have missed a problem.
- After introducing this activity students should be able to work in small groups after completing work. Great for kids that finish work early.

Assessment: Grading should be based on accurately finding solutions and reaching the right color.

NBT.B 2.9 Lesson One

Title: Show Me

Topic: Showing that a problem is solvable

Objective of lesson: Students will demonstrate how to solve a math problem using manipulatives.

Common Core Standard used: NBT.B 2.9: Explain why addition and subtraction strategies work, using place values and the properties of operations

Materials needed:

Blocks

Time for lesson: 5 minutes per person

Lesson:

- Tell students that they are going to help teach today. They need to come up with one math problem with two digit numbers and then either draw or use manipulatives to show others how to solve the problem.
- Allow students to demonstrate their problem.

Assessment: Grading should be based on accurately finding solutions and demonstrating how to arrive at the answer.

NBT.B 2.9 Lesson Two

Title: Two Of A Kind

Topic: Showing that a problem is solvable

Objective of lesson: Students will show one to one correlation to demonstrate different manipulatives can serve the same purpose.

Common Core Standard used: NBT.B 2.9: Explain why addition and subtraction strategies work, using place values and the properties of operations

Materials needed:

Blocks

Crayons

Paper clips

Anything that can be used as a math manipulative

Time for lesson: 5 minutes - per student

Lesson:

- Have students create a unique math problem.
- Allow students to use manipulatives to represent their math problem.
- Have students create a second, different manipulative set to represent the same problem.

Assessment: Grading should be based on accurately finding solutions and demonstrating how to arrive at the answer in two separate manners.

MD.A 2.1 Lesson One

Title: Choose A Tool

Topic: Choosing the correct tool for measuring a given length

Objective of lesson: Students will work in pairs to choose the correct tools for measuring given lengths, then measure those lengths.

Common Core Standard used: MD.A 2.1: Measure the length of an object by selecting and using appropriate tools such as rulers, yardsticks, meter sticks, and measuring tapes.

Materials needed:

Rulers

Yardsticks

Meter sticks

Measuring tape

Lengths of colored string or tape on the floor

Time for lesson: 10-20 minutes

Lesson:

- Explain to students that there are lots of ways to measure an object, ruler, yardstick, meter stick, and more. However, it is hard to measure a line that goes all the way across the room with a regular ruler, a yardstick is a better option.

- Show students the string pieces or the tape on the floor. Allow them to choose a tool and measure each length of string. Have students record the string color, what tool they used, and the measurement.

Assessment: Grading should be based on choosing the correct tool and getting an accurate measurement.

MD.A 2.1 Lesson Two

Title: How Does The Classroom Measure Up?

Topic: Measuring objects with differing tools

Objective of lesson: Students will work in pairs to measure items in the classroom.

Common Core Standard used: MD.A 2.1: Measure the length of an object by selecting and using appropriate tools such as rulers, yardsticks, meter sticks, and measuring tapes.

Materials needed:

Rulers

Yardsticks

Meter sticks

Measuring tape

Index cards

Markers

Time for lesson: 20-30 minutes

Lesson:

- Have students pair up and randomly hand out measuring tools.
- Tell students that they are to find five unique objects in the room that can be appropriately measures with their given instrument.

- Allow students to find, measure, and record object lengths, then label those objects with the lengths.

Assessment: Grading should be based on finding, measuring, and recording five unique objects.

MD.A 2.2 Lesson One

Title: Dual Measures

Topic: Measuring using different units

Objective of lesson: Students will measure objects using inches and centimeters.

Common Core Standard used: MD.A 2.2: Measure the length of an object twice, using length units of different lengths for the two measurements; describe how the two measurements relate to the size of the unit chosen.

Materials needed:

Assortment of small and medium objects

Rulers (marked with centimeters and inches)

Time for lesson: 10-15 minutes

Lesson:

- Allow students to choose three objects to measure.
- Have students write down which object they chose and the measurement in inches and centimeters. Use math journal.
- Ask student which is the smaller unit of measure. How do they know?
- Assessment: Grading should be based on correct measurements in both units.

MD.A 2.2 Lesson Two

Title: Making Wise Choices

Topic: Measuring using different units

Objective of lesson: Students will measure pieces of tape to determine which unit is the best form of measurement.

Common Core Standard used: MD.A 2.2: Measure the length of an object twice, using length units of different lengths for the two measurements; describe how the two measurements relate to the size of the unit chosen.

Materials needed:

Lengths of tape (on the floor, some over three feet with others less than an inch)

Measuring tools with different units

Time for lesson: 10-15 minutes

Lesson: (Small groups)

- Show students the tape on the floor. Explain that they will be measuring each piece of tape, but need to find the best tool.
- Students should work with partners and they should discuss their thoughts and ideas.
- Allow students to use the different tools to measure each piece of tape to decide both length and best tool.

- Once the tool is chosen have students record the actual measurement and unit used.

Assessment: Grading should be based on correct measurements and choice of appropriate tool.

Help students remember measurements by creating mental pictures.

1 inch - a knuckle

1 foot - license plate

1 yard - baseball bat

1 mile - 20 minute walk

1 mm - pencil tip

1 cm - width of finger

1 dc - width of hand

1 m - width of door

1 km - 10 minute walk

MD.A 2.3 Lesson One

Title: Guesstimates

Topic: Estimating different lengths in feet

Objective of lesson: Students will estimate lengths in different units.

Common Core Standard used: MD.A 2.3: Estimate lengths using units of inches, feet, centimeters, and meters.

Materials needed:

Ruler (placed on display)

Several objects, lengths of string, or tape on the floor

Time for lesson: 10-15 minutes

Lesson:

- Show students the ruler and explain that it is exactly 1 foot long.
- Lay the ruler against one of the objects to be measured. Explain that if the ruler is a foot longer than 5 rulers would be five feet long. How many rulers do you think it would take to line up and be the length of (fill in)? After taking guesses, actually measure to show who was closest.
- Allow students to estimate other object lengths in feet and then measure as a class to see who was closest.

Assessment: Grading should be based on legitimate estimates.

MD.A 2.3 Lesson Two

Title: Just Inching Along

Topic: Estimating different lengths in inches

Objective of lesson: Students will estimate lengths in different units

Common Core Standard used: MD.A 2.3: Estimate lengths using units of inches, feet, centimeters, and meters.

Materials needed:

Selection of small toys and blocks

Index cards

Ruler

Time for lesson: 10-15 minutes

Lesson: (Small groups)

- Line up several small toys on a flat surface in front of the group. Show the group how long an inch is on the ruler.
- Tell them without using the ruler they should estimate how tall each toy is. Record their estimates on index cards.
- Now have students decide which toys could be lined up, end to end, to reach a certain number of inches. Actually measure to see how close the estimates were.

Assessment: Grading should be based on legitimate estimates and participation.

MD.A 2.4 Lesson One

Title: How Do I Measure Up?

Topic: Measuring and comparing different lengths

Objective of lesson: Students will measure different length objects

Common Core Standard used: MD.A 2.4: Measure to determine how much longer one object is than another, expressing the length difference in terms of a standard length unit.

Materials needed:

Ruler/Yard stick/Growth chart

Marker

Time for lesson: 45-60 minutes

Lesson:

- Tell students they are going to practice measuring using each other as objects.
- Have students lie on the floor and get measured by a partner or stand against a growth chart if one is available.
- Mark or record each student's height and name.
- Next have students decide who is tallest, shortest, and (time permitting) where each individual falls on the chart, who is the sixth tallest? The next to shortest?

Assessment: Grading should be based on participation and accurate measurements.

MD.A 2.4 Lesson Two

Title: Scavenger Hunt

Topic: Measuring and comparing different lengths

Objective of lesson: Students will measure different length objects to find particular lengths

Common Core Standard used: MD.A 2.4: Measure to determine how much longer one object is than another, expressing the length difference in terms of a standard length unit.

Materials needed:

Rulers (per student)

Scavenger list (Sample included)

Timer

Time for lesson: 15-20 minutes

Lesson:

- Offer every student a ruler and explain that they are going to go on a measurement scavenger hunt in the classroom.
- Offer students the included scavenger hunt list.
- Allow students a set amount of time to find as many objects as possible on the scavenger list. Each object is a certain length, students must measure to find an object that is that length then record what they found.

Assessment: Grading should be based on accurate measurements and participating in the scavenger hunt.

Scavenger Hunt:

Find an object in the classroom that is the following measurement. Record the name of the object you found.

1) 1 inch

2) 5 inches

3) 1 foot

4) 6 $\frac{1}{2}$ inches

5) 15 inches

6) 2 inches

7) 3 inches

8) 11 inches

9) 2 feet

10) 7 $\frac{1}{2}$ inches

MD.B 2.5 Lesson One

Title: Measure Your Words

Topic: Word problems involving length

Objective of lesson: Students will accurately solve word problems about length.

Common Core Standard used: MD.B 2.5: Use addition and subtraction within 100 to solve word problems involving lengths that are given in the same units, e.g., by using drawings (such as drawings of rulers) and equations with a symbol for the unknown number to represent the problem.

Materials needed:

Worksheet (Included)

Manipulatives

Time for lesson: 20-30 minutes

Lesson:

- Review previous lessons that relate.
- Students can review with small groups.
- Students should create their own ideas and write in their math journals.
- Have students complete the included worksheet by solving, through the use of rulers or other manipulatives as needed.

Assessment: Grading should be based on accurate answers.

Measure Your Words Worksheet:

1) If I have a piece of string that is 3 inches long and I lay it end to end with Sarah's piece of string that is 5 inches long, how many inches of string will we have together?

____

2) I am making something for an arts and crafts fair that requires yarn. I have 6 inches of yarn in my bag, but I need 15 inches total. How much more yarn do I need to buy?

____

3) I am growing out my hair for Locks of Love. They use human hair to make wigs for people who lose their hair when they have cancer. I am willing to get my hair cut pretty short, but I need 14 inches of hair to cut off. I am to the point that I can cut 11 inches off. How many more inches of hair will I have to wait to grow before I can donate it?

____

4) I am 2 feet 6 inches tall. I hope to be the same height as my mother who is 5 feet 6 inches tall. How many more feet will I have to grow to be the same height as my mother?

____

MD.B 2.5 Lesson Two

Title: Follow The Rulers

Topic: Word problems involving length

Objective of lesson: Students will accurately solve word problems about length.

Common Core Standard used: MD.B 2.5: Use addition and subtraction within 100 to solve word problems involving lengths that are given in the same units, e.g., by using drawings (such as drawings of rulers) and equations with a symbol for the unknown number to represent the problem.

Materials needed:

Worksheet (Included)

Paper rulers
(http://www.mrmyers.org/Teacher_Resources/rulers.html)

Time for lesson: 10-15 minutes

Lesson:

- Have students solve the included problems, in word problem form.
- Once the answer is solved, have students mark the right answer on the ruler. Have them number the mark to correspond with the problem.

Assessment: Grading should be based on accurate answers and correct marking on a ruler.

Word Problems:

1) When wrapping a gift I first tear off 3 inches of tape for the top. This is never enough so I tear off another 7 inches to tape down both sides. I always need a bow, so I add another inch of tape to hold it on. How many inches of tape are used to wrap my gift? ______________

2) I had 12 inches of string and four kittens. The first kitten took 2 inches to play with. The second kitten only took 1 inch. The third and fourth kitten took 6 inches to share. How much string do I have left?

____

3) When hanging curtains, the length is very important. I have enough material to make curtains that are 45 inches long, but I only need curtains that are 38 inches long. How much material can I cut off?

____

4) I am braiding my own bracelet. When you braid a bracelet, the string gets shorter. I am starting with 36 inches of string. When I am finished the bracelet will be 10 inches long. How much shorter does braiding make the string? __________________

5) I have three little dogs that came with a play set. Each has a small plastic leash. Two of the leashes are 2 inches long and the third is three inches long. If I laid them end to end, how long would they be?

____

MD.B 2.6 Lesson One

Title: Make Me A Ruler

Topic: Representing whole numbers as lengths

Objective of lesson: Students will create a ruler from memory

Common Core Standard used: MD.B 2.6: Represent whole numbers as lengths from 0 on a number line diagram with equally spaced points corresponding to the numbers 0, 1, 2, ..., and represent whole-number sums and differences within 100 on a number line diagram.

Materials needed:

Paper strips

Pencils

Time for lesson: 20-35 minutes

Lesson:

- Ask students what the specific characteristics of a ruler are. Things such as have marks, have numbers, and are equally spaced are important. Review measurements.
- Tell students that they are going to make their own ruler with these traits and though you know the measurements will not be exact, they should try to mark the ruler appropriately and number each inch. Have students work in small groups.

Assessment: Grading should be based on valid guesses at marking, even spacing, and appropriate numbering.

MD.B 2.6 Lesson Two

Title: Ruled Out

Topic: Representing lengths as whole numbers

Objective of lesson: Students will number a ruler from memory

Common Core Standard used: MD.B 2.6: Represent whole numbers as lengths from 0 on a number line diagram with equally spaced points corresponding to the numbers 0, 1, 2, ..., and represent whole-number sums and differences within 100 on a number line diagram.

Materials needed:

Ruler sections worksheet (Included)

Pencils

Time for lesson: 5-10 minutes

Lesson:

- Explain to students that all rulers look different, some are made from different materials, and others have numbers that have been skipped.
- Tell students that they will have to look carefully, but they are to fill in the missing numbers for each ruler.

Assessment: Grading should be based on appropriate renumbering

1 3 4 6

HTTP://WWW.DADS
FREE MATH WORKS
IMPERIAL INCHES

4 5 7 8

HTTP://WWW.DADSWORKSHEETS.COM
FREE MATH WORKSHEETS SINCE 2008

8 9 11 12

SWORKSHEETS.COM
SHEETS SINCE 2008
MADE IN U.S.A.

1 4 5 6

HTTP://WWW.DADS
FREE MATH WORKS
IMPERIAL INCHES

5 6 7 9

HTTP://WWW.DADSWORKSHEETS.COM
FREE MATH WORKSHEETS SINCE 2008

7 10 12

SWORKSHEETS.COM
SHEETS SINCE 2008
MADE IN U.S.A.

MD.C 2.7 Lesson One

Title: Tick Tock

Topic: Telling time with technology

Objective of lesson: Students will set an analog clock to a given time

Common Core Standard used: MD.C 2.7: Tell and write time from analog and digital clocks to the nearest five minutes, using a.m. and p.m.

Materials needed:

Computer access with Internet

Time for lesson: 30-40 minutes

Lesson: (Pairs)

- Help students to log onto to http://www.sheppardsoftware.com/mathgames/earlymath/on_time_game1.htm
- Allow students to work in pairs, taking turns at each level to see who can set the time correctly in the least amount of time.
- Have students alert you to their scores at each level.
- Great activity when students finish work early.

Assessment: Grading should be based on scores through the program.

MD.C 2.7 Lesson Two

Title: Night And Day

Topic: A.M. and P.M.

Objective of lesson: Students will note a.m. or p.m. as appropriate.

Common Core Standard used: MD.C 2.7: Tell and write time from analog and digital clocks to the nearest five minutes, using a.m. and p.m.

Materials needed:

Schedule of events (Sample included)

Markers

Time for lesson: 10-15 minutes

Lesson:

- Explain to students that you wrote out a list of activities you had to do with the times, but forgot whether to mark them AM or PM. This is confusing because you do not know what should be completed in the morning and what should be finished at night.
- Share the randomized schedule with students.
- Have students help you decide whether the activities should be marked AM or PM based on when they should happen.
- Students should create their own- with answers in their math journals.

Assessment: Grading should be based on correctly identifying AM and PM. *Can make miniature versions of the schedule to allow individuals to work alone.

Get Out of Bed	6:00
Eat Lunch	12:00
Eat Breakfast	8:00
Brush Teeth	8:15
Go to Work	9:00
Walk the Dog	5:00
Play Video Games	6:00
Read a Book	10:00
Go to Bed	11:00

MD.C 2.8 Lesson One

Title: That Makes Cents

Topic: Solving word problems related to money

Objective of lesson: Students will solve word problems containing information about cents (pennies, nickels, dines, and quarters)

Common Core Standard used: MD.C 2.8: Solve word problems involving dollar bills, quarters, dimes, nickels, and pennies, using $ and ¢ symbols appropriately. Example: If you have 2 dimes and 3 pennies, how many cents do you have?

Materials needed:

Change (plastic math money)

Time for lesson: 20-30 minutes

Lesson:

- Hand out a worksheet and plastic 'change' to each student.
- Explain that there are many times in life in which we must make change so we need to know what each is worth.
- Have students solve problems by counting the change in front of them.

Assessment: Grading should be based on correctly answering word problems.

Sample Problems:

1) If I have 1 quarter and 2 dimes, how many cents to I have? ______

2) If you have 2 dimes, 6 pennies, and a nickel, how many cents do you have? _______

3) If you have 7 pennies and a quarter, how many cents do you have?

____

4) If I have 5 dimes and 10 nickels, how many cents do I have?_______

5) If I have 10 cents and give someone five of it, what do I have left?_______

6) If you have two quarters and 3 pennies, how many cents do you have? ______

7) If you have 1 nickel, 1 dime, 1 quarter, and 1 penny, how many cents do you have? ________

8) If I have 1 quarter and 2 nickels, how many cents do I have?

____

9) If I have 9 dimes, how many cents do I have? _____

10) If I have 11 pennies, 2 nickels, and 1 quarter, how many cents do I have? _________

MD.C 2.8 Lesson Two

Title: Making Changes

Topic: Solving problems related to money

Objective of lesson: Students will solve real life examples involving money.

Common Core Standard used: MD.C 2.8: Solve word problems involving dollar bills, quarters, dimes, nickels, and pennies, using $ and ¢ symbols appropriately. Example: If you have 2 dimes and 3 pennies, how many cents do you have?

Materials needed:

Change (plastic math money)

Time for lesson: 10-15 minutes -each small group

Lesson: (Small groups)

- Have plastic money set out in front of students. Allow students to have only the change as the teacher holds the dollars.
- Give students one verbal problem at a time: Let's pretend you sold me a small toy for 54 cents and I gave you a dollar. See if you can give me the correct change. (If necessary tell students how much change is owed)
- Have students create their own problems - math journal.

Assessment: Grading should be based on correctly answering verbal word problems.

MD.D 2.9 Lesson One

Title: Taking Graphing Measures

Topic: Line plots

Objective of lesson: Students will create a line graph based on taken measurements.

Common Core Standard used: MD.D 2.9: Generate measurement data by measuring lengths of several objects to the nearest whole unit, or by making repeated measurements of the same object. Show the measurements by making a line plot, where the horizontal scale is marked off in whole-number units.

Materials needed:

Graph paper

Rulers

Assortment of blocks

Time for Lesson: 15-20 minutes

Lesson:

- Allow each student to choose two or three blocks and a ruler.
- Have students measure and then write down the length of each of their blocks.
- Demonstrate how to create a line plot on paper. Have students number horizontally using whole numbers.

- Then poll the entire class to determine how many x's belong above each line.
- Have students label the horizontal axis.

Assessment: Grading should be based on correctly creating and filling in the graph.

Sample:

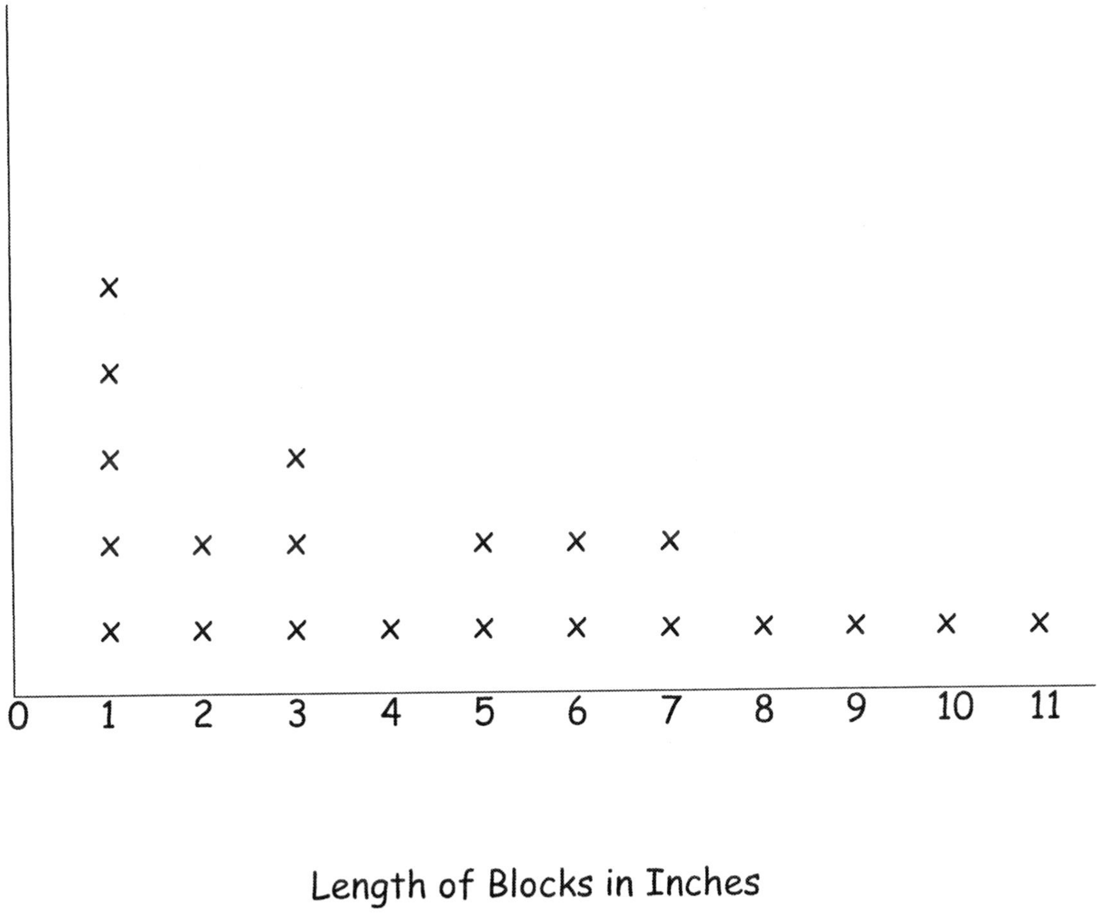

0 1 2 3 4 5 6 7 8 9 10 11

Length of Blocks in Inches

MD.D 2.9 Lesson Two

Title: Ask Around

Topic: Line Plot

Objective of lesson: Students will create a line graph based on information gathered from classmates.

Common Core Standard used: MD.D 2.9: Generate measurement data by measuring lengths of several objects to the nearest whole unit, or by making repeated measurements of the same object. Show the measurements by making a line plot, where the horizontal scale is marked off in whole-number units.

Materials needed:

Graph paper

List of people in class and two columns on a paper (brothers/sisters)

Time for Lesson: 15-20 minutes

Lesson:

- Have students poll everyone in the class to find out if they have brothers or sister and how many they have of each.
- Allow students to record student responses on their sheet.
- Next have students create two line plot graphs, one for brothers, one for sister. *Remind students to include themselves.

Assessment: Grading should be based on correctly creating and filling in the graph.

MD.D 2.10 Lesson One

Title: Weather Or Not To Record

Topic: Bar graphs

Objective of lesson: Students will create a bar graph over time about weather

Common Core Standard used: MD.D 2.10: Draw a picture graph and a bar graph (with single-unit scale) to represent a data set with up to four categories. Solve simple put-together, take-apart, and compare problems[1] using information presented in a bar graph.

Materials needed:

Graph paper

Colored pencils

Lesson: (Long term lesson)

- Explain to students that you are going to create a bar graph, but to create a bar graph you must have lots of information.
- Tell students that they are going to be the ones to gather information for this project. Together, list all the types of weather that can be expected during the data gathering period.
- List these weather types at the bottom of a graph, with number of days on the vertical axis (sample included)
- Each day have a student check the weather and share with the class what data to add to the graph.

- Show students how to add a section to their graph over time.

Assessment: Grading should be based on correctly creating and filling in the graph.

- Make sure students include the following:
- create a name for the graph
- name x axis and y axis
- appropriate scale and interval

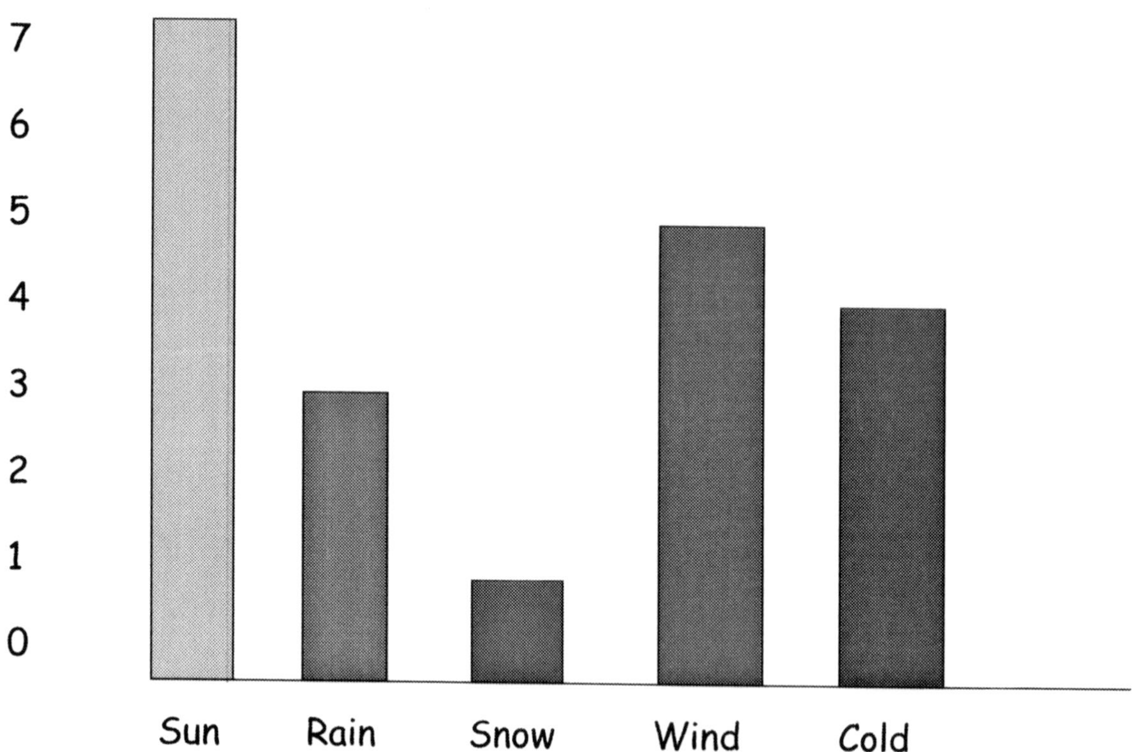

MD.D 2.10 Lesson Two

Title: Favorite Foods

Topic: Picture graphs

Objective of lesson: Students help to create a picture graph about the class's favorite foods

Common Core Standard used: MD.D 2.10: Draw a picture graph and a bar graph (with single-unit scale) to represent a data set with up to four categories. Solve simple put-together, take-apart, and compare problems[1] using information presented in a bar graph.

Materials needed:

Pictures (of top five favorite food in the class)

Velcro or tape

Projector

Transparent graph

Time for Lesson: 20-30 minutes

Lesson:

- Explain to students that you are going to make a unique type of graph called a picture graph. Picture graphs are just what they sound like, graphs made of pictures.
- Have students come up one at a time and choose which food (of the ones given) they enjoy the most.

- As the large graph is projected on the wall, have students place their 'favorite' into the right column.
- Have students create a picture graph of their own, a topic of their choosing, with at least three columns. Pictures can be drawn in as they interview at least ten people in class to help fill in their graph.
- Allow plenty of time for the full project.

Assessment: Grading should be based on correctly creating and filling in the graph. Students should include a key.

Favorite Foods Graph

Pizza Hamburgers Chicken Vegetables Fruit

G.A 2.1 Lesson One

Title: Mystery Shape

Topic: Identifying shapes with specific attributes

Objective of lesson: Students identify shapes given only certain attributes.

Common Core Standard used: G.A 2.1: Recognize and draw shapes having specified attributes, such as a given number of angles or a given number of equal faces. Identify triangles, quadrilaterals, pentagons, hexagons, and cubes.

Materials needed:

Paper

Pencils

Clues (Samples included)

Time for Lesson: 15-20 minutes

Lesson:

- Have students fold a sheet of paper so that 6 squares are created (fold in thirds and then in half)
- Next, read clues one at a time. As students hear the clue they should draw the shape being described. Have students draw across the top row and then the bottom.
- Students can add to shapes and names to their math journal.

Assessment: Grading should be based on the number of correctly drawn shapes.

Sample Clues:

1) I have three angles and when I am drawn flat I have a single face, but make me 3D and I have at least four faces. (triangle/pyramid)

2) I have no angles, but I am always on a roll. (circle)

3) Six faces, four angles on each face, building with me takes lots of space. (cube)

4) Eight sides and eight angles, I will stop before I say too much. (octagon)

5) Five sides, five angles, you may live in a 3D version of me. There is even a famous building made in my shape. (pentagon)

6) Almost a circle, but not quite there. I wobble when I roll but I just don't care. (oval)

G.A 2.1 Lesson Two

Title: We're Going On A Shape Hunt

Topic: Identifying items with specific shapes

Objective of lesson: Students identify items with specific shapes

Common Core Standard used: G.A 2.1: Recognize and draw shapes having specified attributes, such as a given number of angles or a given number of equal faces. Identify triangles, quadrilaterals, pentagons, hexagons, and cubes.

Materials needed:

Baskets labeled with shape names

Time for Lesson: 20-30 minutes (per group)

Lesson: (Small group)

- Explain to students that shapes are seen in everything we use and see daily, but many times we just don't pay attention.
- Have students to choose a basket to carry, this is not the only shape they will search for, but it is the basket they will carry.
- Take students on a shape walk around the room until several shapes have been found by each student. If you can go outside that is even better.

Assessment: Grading should be based on locating items of expected shapes.

G.A 2.2 Lesson One

Title: Know When To Fold Them

Topic: Partitioning rectangles

Objective of lesson: Students will partition a sheet of paper into equal sections, then count the sections

Common Core Standard used: G.A 2.2: Partition a rectangle into rows and columns of same-size squares and count to find the total number of them.

Materials needed:

Drawing paper

Time for Lesson: 5-10 minutes

Lesson:

- Tell students you are going to do some paper folding today.
- Have students fold the full sheet in half-length wise (hotdog). Demonstrate if necessary.
- Now have students make six equal folds the other direction, then count the number of squares that are created.
- Continue practicing before any lessons. Great review.

Assessment: Grading should be based on folding correctly and counting correctly.

G.A 2.2 Lesson Two

Title: Make Me Equal

Topic: Partitioning rectangles

Objective of lesson: Students will partition a sheet of paper into equal sections

Common Core Standard used: G.A 2.2: Partition a rectangle into rows and columns of same-size squares and count to find the total number of them.

Materials needed:

Drawing paper (several sheets for each student)

Time for Lesson: 5-10 minutes

Lesson: (small groups)

- Have students put their thinking caps on as you hand each the first sheet of paper.
- Ask students to fold a sheet of paper evenly to create 10 equal squares, then 12 equal squares, then 4 equal squares, etc.

Assessment: Grading should be based on folding equally and counting correctly.

G.A 2.3 Lesson One

Title: Shape Up

Topic: Partitioning shapes equally

Objective of lesson: Students will partition shapes equally.

Common Core Standard used: G.A 2.3: Partition circles and rectangles into two, three, or four equal shares, describe the shares using the words halves, thirds, half of, a third of, etc., and describe the whole as two halves, three thirds, four fourths. Recognize that equal shares of identical wholes need not have the same shape.

Materials needed:

Paper circles and rectangles for each student

Time for Lesson: 15-20 minutes

Lesson: (small groups)

- Have students cut out shapes if necessary.
- Explain to students squares are not the only shapes that can be folded in equal parts.
- Have students fold the shapes in a given number of equal sections.
- Explain to students that by counting the sections we can learn how many part the whole has at the time. So three folds mean it

is folded in thirds, four equal parts mean it is folded in fourths, etc. This can be expanded to introduce fractions.

- Have students color a fraction of the shape and label each part.

Assessment: Grading should be based on folding equally and basic participation.

G.A 2.3 Lesson Two

Title: Parts Of A Whole

Topic: Understanding parts make a whole

Objective of lesson: Students will understand that parts can equal a whole.

Common Core Standard used: G.A 2.3: Partition circles and rectangles into two, three, or four equal shares, describe the shares using the words halves, thirds, half of, a third of, etc., and describe the whole as two halves, three thirds, four fourths. Recognize that equal shares of identical wholes need not have the same shape.

Materials needed:

Paper circles and rectangles for each student

Scissors

Time for Lesson: 10-15 minutes

Lesson: (small groups)

- Have students cut out several of each shape to work with.
- Have students cut a rectangle into six equal sections, and a circle into four equal sections. Have another rectangle cut into six equal sections and a circle into eight equal sections.
- Have students reassemble the shapes. One shape at a time have students count how many sections are there. Explain that that is

the whole, it equals one so if it has 8 sections then 8/8 is the same as one; 6 sections 6/6 equals one.

- Next show students how to show fractions, the whole number will always be on the bottom and how ever many pieces are there will go on top. So if a shape has six sections and we remove two we have 4/6 left. Though it is read as 4/6ths it can be remembered as 4 out/of 6.
- Repeat with various shapes and fractions.

Assessment: Grading should be based on being able to tell you how many parts are in each whole and represent $\frac{1}{2}$, $\frac{3}{4}$, etc.

Sample shapes

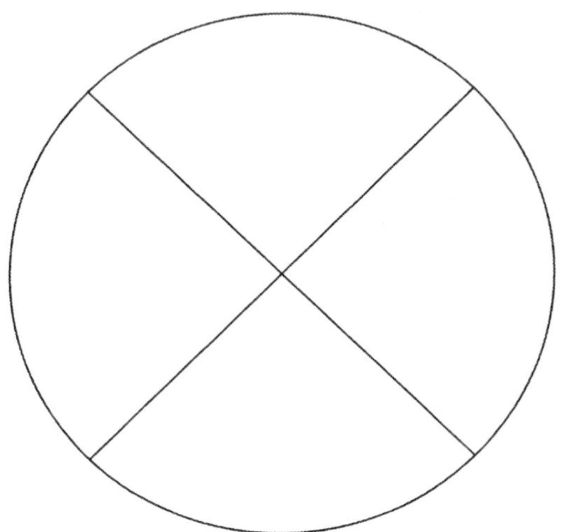

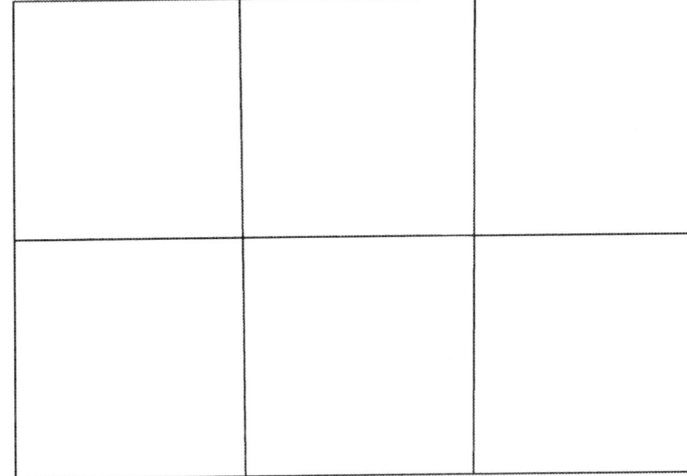